Memories of a Maplewood Boyhood

Joseph K. Newman

To order additional copies of this book, contact:
Xlibris Corporation
1-888-795-4274
www.Xlibris.com
Orders@Xlibris.com
36618

CONTENTS

Foreword 9

Early Years 11

School Days 35

The Family 89

Some Other Memories 109

Random Recollections 121

Excerpts from my 1946, ninth-grade diary 131

Al and Dottie Newman—Wedding Day, June 22, 1930

This book is dedicated to my parents,
Al and Dottie Newman,
without whom I would not have had a Maplewood boyhood.

FOREWORD

On many occasions during my life I have wondered what daily life was like for my grandparents growing up in the Newark and New York of the 1880s and 1890s. What was it like at home, at school, in the neighborhood? What did Joe Kussy, Josie Hertz, Harold Newman and Dora Axelroth (my grandparents) do and think about during their growing up years?

As an amateur historian and as a curious grandson (now seventy-five years of age and a grandfather of five myself) I would dearly like to know, but it's just not possible; none of my grandparents ever wrote down anything about his or her early life (or if they did, none of it has survived). Fortunately, my maternal great aunt, Sarah Kussy, a teacher in the Newark public schools for almost a half century, did write a "family chronicle" memoir about the Kussy family's history and experiences in Newark from their early days in America in the 1850s until about the turn of that century. Aunt Sarah's memoir provided some interesting information, just enough to whet my appetite for more—much more. Sadly, that appetite will remain unfulfilled.

I don't want that to be the case for my own children and grandchildren. I hope they will be interested to read something about what my life and the lives of my family members and contemporaries were like in the Maplewood of the 1930s and 1940s. Thus this little memoir.

I apologize in advance for any errors stemming from imperfect memory or inadvertence on my part.

EARLY YEARS

The Neighborhood

Social Structure

The Village

Local Stores

My earliest years—Clinton Avenue, Newark. I was born on March 26, 1931, on my father's twenty-seventh birthday, at Beth Israel Hospital in Newark, New Jersey. For the record, my father was born on March 26, 1904 and my mother on May 28, 1907, both also in Newark. My first home was in the town house of my grandparents, Dr. Joseph Kussy and Josephine Hertz Kussy. This was a four story (plus basement) house at number 82 Clinton Avenue, Newark. The ground floor was my grandfather's dental office suite (he was an oral surgeon/exodontist, a graduate of the University of Pennsylvania Dental College, Class of 1898), consisting of waiting room, surgery, nurse's office, recovery room and lavatory. On the second floor were my grandparents' living room, dining room, kitchen and a bathroom. The third floor contained my grandparents' sitting room, bedroom and a bathroom. On the top floor were my bedroom, my parents' bedroom and a bathroom. Such was my little kingdom during my first few years of life.

My parents of course paid rent, without doubt quite a modest sum, the years 1931-34 being the worst years of the Great Depression. Certainly my dad wasn't making very much money then. He worked as a commercial real estate broker in the firm of Feist & Feist. The commercial real estate business was in terrible doldrums in those years, but my father just managed to arrange enough store leasing deals to make ends meet for the young Newman family.

How wonderful it was to have loving parents and doting grandparents during my first few years. I have always thanked God for my great good fortune in being born to Al and Dottie Newman, the world's finest, most wonderful parents for as long as they lived and now in my heart and mind forever. And the same goes for my grandparents, known from the very beginning to me and my sister Rhoda as "Pa" and "Nanna."

I have only a few memories of those years. My crib was near the window, which looked out over Clinton Avenue below. Looking out early in the morning, I would see the men who shoveled the horse dung from the streets (there were still many horse-drawn vehicles in those years). The men had large garbage pails on wheels, into which they would shovel the dung. I would also see the coming of the milkman and the iceman. This was before the advent of mechanical refrigerators, and my grandparents then had what was called an "ice box". Interestingly, even after the advent of the refrigerator, we still for years referred to the latter as the "ice box." The other things I would see as I gazed down from my perch at the wonders of the world were automobiles and my great favorites, the electric trolley cars, clanging along their tracks.

The two people who awakened the earliest at No. 82 were Nanna and I. Nanna would come up and collect me from my crib and carry me down to her floor. She would make coffee and toast and I would "dunk" my buttered toast, often cinnamon toast (butter, sugar and cinnamon and delicious!), in her coffee before eating it. How I loved this delightful morning ritual! To this day I love to dunk.

I remember the basement as a dark and scary place. There was of course a coal room, into which the coal delivery man would send the coal by means of a chute leading down into the coal bin. The furnace-stoking was the job of Pa's colored "handy man" ("colored" or "Negro" was the correct term to use in those days; neither was pejorative), but if he wasn't around when the furnace needed stoking, Pa or my dad would do the shoveling.

The house had a smallish backyard surrounded by wooden fencing. I used to play there on fine days, mostly in summer of course. Once I even had a little vegetable garden, which was planted and tended by our colored maid, Emma, whom I liked very much. My own contribution to the garden work was watering it, using an old-fashioned kind of watering pail made of light metal. Emma liked me too and was always very nice to me. Once she took me to her home, which wasn't very far away, to show me off to her own family.

It was during these Clinton Avenue years that I first learned about God. My grandparents and parents gave me the knowledge that there is a God, that He created the universe and all the people and creatures in it, that He watched over it and us, and that His place was in Heaven up above the Earth, where His people lived. I remember my early and imperfect comprehension of these concepts of God, Heaven and Earth. Clinton Avenue was the part of Earth that I knew from my own personal observation. On Clinton Avenue across the street from our house, and a short distance down that then quite attractive thoroughfare, there was a drugstore named Linnett's. For some reason, whenever I pictured God, I saw Him up above Linnett's, perhaps a hundred yards above. I saw Him as a large, disembodied head in the clouds, gazing down upon His creation, the Earth and His people, which I knew included me.

When I was about three years old, my parents taught me my first prayer, which I was to say to God every night before going to sleep. It went as follows:

"God bless Daddy, Mommy and Rhoda, Pa and Nanna, Grandpa and Grandma, and all my aunts and uncles and cousins and friends. Amen."

Why do I remember the words so exactly? Because I have repeated them almost every night ever since!

Verona Days. When I was four years old, we moved from 82 Clinton Avenue to Verona, a suburb a few miles out on Bloomfield Avenue. There we lived in a nice two-story frame house on a quiet street. I have only a few recollections of my life there.

I made my first friend there, a neighbor my age named Louise Gartley, known to the street as "Ouisie" (pronounced "Weezee"). Ouisie and I used to sit on a low branch of the apple tree in our backyard and eat Ovaltine out of its famous cylindrical container. Alas, when we moved from Verona, I lost touch with my friend and never saw her again. I hope she had a good, happy and rewarding life.

Behind our small backyard was a huge—so it seemed to me—area which I think was part of the property our rented house was on. It was an area with many fruit trees and berry bushes. I distinctly recall being back there one day with my grandfather Newman, picking blackberries which we consumed that very day and which were quite delicious. We also picked apples from our apple trees.

Finally, I can recall often going around the corner with my mother, accompanied of course by sister Rho in her stroller, to the grocery store nearby. Once my mother made me a basket of vegetables, the centerpiece of which was an eggplant, which I found most fascinating and beautiful. I carried this basket around with me for several days, most proudly.

Johnson Avenue, Newark. After a one-year residence in our rented house in Verona from the summer of 1934 through the summer of 1935, we moved to Newark and settled into an apartment on Johnson Avenue across and down the street from my Kussy grandparents' apartment building, the Ambassador, to which they had moved after selling 82 Clinton Avenue. The reason we moved back, i.e., the reason my mother gave to her friends and acquaintances, was that she was homesick for her parents. She had after all lived with them all her life, including during the first four years of her married life. So indeed she may have been somewhat homesick, but that was not the principal reason why we left our nice little Verona house with its wonderful fruit orchard and berry patches in the back. In fact we moved mainly for the following reason. My father's compensation in the Feist & Feist real estate firm, where he worked, was based entirely on commissions earned. Such commissions were hardly bountiful in the Depression year 1935, so it was not at all certain that we would be able to buy coal to heat the Verona house during the winter of 1935-36, whereas heat was included in the monthly rent of the Johnson Avenue apartment.

The year we lived there, before our move to Maplewood, was the only time in their married life—until they retired to Florida in the 1960s—that my parents lived in an apartment.

I remember nothing of the actual apartment in which we lived, although I do have recollections of the building itself. What I do remember is that we saw a lot of my grandparents that year and indeed during all the years prior to my going off to university. It was during our year on Johnson Avenue that my grandparents gave me "Eggy," my favorite stuffed animal, a yellow and brown dog which I have to this day.

They also gave me a shoeshine kit, complete with brush, buffing cloth and polish ("Griffin" brand in those days). One day I noticed that the "super" of our apartment building was wearing black boots that were covered with dust. I offered to give him a shine. In fact all I did was brush the dust off his boots. For this he gave me a dime, which my mother promptly made me give back to him. In those days a dime had a purchasing power of more than two dollars in current dollars so my mother was quite right in making me give it back.

I kept and used this shoeshine kit for many years, until I entered the U.S. Foreign Service and went to my first foreign posting, Paris, in 1961.

Colgate Road Years. We moved to 21 Colgate Road in 1937, after living in a rented "bungalow" on Boyden Avenue in Maplewood for one year, where and when I attended kindergarten at Clinton School. The houses on Colgate Road were built during the 1920s and each house was different. When we moved there, there were some twenty-seven houses on the street, and one more house was built directly opposite ours shortly after our arrival. At the bottom of the street there were two vacant lots adjoining Springfield Avenue. These lots ran all the way across to Rutgers Street to the west and Wellesley Street to the east. Only one tiny structure stood on the lots, a White Castle hamburger place at the corner of Springfield Avenue and Rutgers Street, where I consumed literally hundreds of five-cent hamburgers over the years (and they were delicious, I should add). Naturally we kids used to play various kinds of games in the lots. During the Second World War, they were perfect sites for us kids' mock battles, commando raids, ambushes and such. They were also perfect sites for grasshopper hunting. What made the lots particularly appealing to us was that they were totally untended and therefore quite densely overgrown with trees, bushes, tall grasses and weeds.

The Great Colgate Road Fire. Whenever the weather was dry for an extended period, the vegetation in the lots dried out to tinderbox condition. One fine day during such a dry spell (I'm not sure of the year—some time in 1941 or 1942, I think), possessed by some kind of demon (fortunately only temporarily), I took a pack of matches from our house and walked alone down to the lot on the west side of Colgate Road, the one we used to cut through on our way to and from Tuscan School. About in the middle of the lot I struck a match and dropped it. It went out. I struck and dropped another. Again no result. On my third try, the dry grass/weeds/brush began to burn, which is what I wanted to see. Okay, I had seen it; now stamp out the fire, Joe. Too late! Despite my attempts to put it out, the fire spread rapidly and quite soon became a nice little conflagration. I realized I had better get out of there like the proverbial bat out of hell and I did so, returning home unseen by any of our neighbors. My heart was beating at quite a pace and I was really "scairt!"

It wasn't long before I heard the wailing sirens of trucks from the Maplewood Fire Department. I emerged from our house and saw neighbors, including many kids, coming out of their houses and heading down Colgate Road to the fire. I joined them. When I arrived down at the lot, about half of it was ablaze. The firemen deployed their hoses and sprayed water onto the flames to the encouraging cheers of the spectators. I watched the proceedings in a perfectly innocent manner. After a time, I heard someone say, "I'll bet that little Benny Benedict started this fire." The neighbor standing next to this accuser agreed. Benny Benedict was a fresh and feisty little guy, perhaps three years younger than I, who lived two houses up from the burning lot. He was known on the street as a little hell-raiser, a brat, a "naughty boy." I on the other hand was universally regarded as a "good boy." It didn't take long for a general consensus to be formed by the spectators that little Benny, who was not even present, had done the deed, which of course demonstrates clearly the importance of one's reputation—good or bad. Did I step forward and set things right by admitting my guilt? I wish I could say that I had done so but alas I did not. Later poor Benny protested his innocence, but who believed him? Only me!

The Benedict family moved away not long after this incident. Wherever you are, Benny, I'm sorry I let you take the blame. And I hope you have had a good life! Eventually I did confess my guilt to my mother and sister—thirty years later!

The Neighborhood. Let us now take a "walk" up and down our street and have a "look" at the families who lived on Colgate Road in our day. Starting on our side, at the bottom of the street, was a family named Ward, who had a daughter named Mary Catherine. Next to them were the Benedicts, with the aforementioned Benny. After the Benedicts moved away, early on, the Greenfield family moved in, with daughter Marjorie, a string bean, a friend of my sister Rho. Next came the Hollanders, with two boys. One was Dickey, with whom I was somewhat friendly. He had an older brother Gene, who later called himself Gino when he became a successful painter. Next door was the Fertell family, with a son named Paul, two years older than I and definitely not the kind of rough and ready athletic type that I aspired to be or to hang out with. After the Fertell house came that of the Toplanskys, with much older daughter Evelyn and son Billy, a few years older than I, whom I looked up to in some ways. Billy had a good collection of baseball cards and got me started collecting them in 1941. When the United States entered the war, he entered the army. Since Billy used to wear a pilot's cap of 1930s vintage (also World War II style) and was nuts about aviation, I had thought he would of course join the Army Air Corps. I was rather disappointed when he became just a plain G.I. I should mention one thing about Mr. Toplansky. He used to actually appear outside wearing only a sleeveless undershirt instead of a shirt (he *did* wear trousers, though). Even at a tender age, I thought that was pretty bad. (Of course, my own dad was always very well dressed, of which we were very proud).

Next door to us, at 23 Colgate Road, lived a family composed of Mr. and Mrs. Schmidt (first names forgotten, if ever known), their adult daughter Edna Schmidt Hummel and her red haired daughter, Betty Hummel, who was a few years older than I. I never knew nor, come to think of it, thought to ask why there was no Mr. Hummel there. Was Mrs. Hummel divorced, widowed, abandoned? The Schmidts were quite old, even very old, in our eyes, in the way that, from the viewpoint of us children looking at them, grandparents always seemed "old" whether they were in their fifties or their eighties. I think the Schmidts were closer to the latter than to the former age group. They were very nice people, although this did not mean that they refrained from scolding me when our backyard baseball or football action extended beyond the boundary of our driveway onto the Schmidt/Hummel backyard. Mom frequently had to caution me, "Don't play in Mrs. Hummel's backyard."

Mr. Schmidt had a bit of a "crush" on my mother, and he liked to kid her about this or that in a gruff voice that he sometimes put on for effect. Mom would address him as "Smitty," which he very much liked, I am sure. Whenever it snowed, he would push the snow off of our sidewalk as well as his own. I say "push" the snow, rather than "shovel," because he didn't use a snow shovel. He had a home-made implement consisting of a rectangular piece of wood with a long wooden handle fitted to it diagonally, and with this he would simply push the snow off the sidewalk. During the course of a heavy snowstorm, he would do this several times, because his implement would only work when the snow was not more than two or three inches high.

Mr. Schmidt had four cars, and all four he somehow fit into his two-car garage. The prize was a Stanley Steamer dating from early in the century. As the name implies, it ran on steam instead of gasoline. Moreover, it really worked, and from time to time he would give us rides on it, which was a thrill and a delight for us. There was also a cute little British Austin. Where, when and why he had acquired this we knew not, nor did we ask. Bear in mind that in the 1930s and 1940s foreign cars were most rare in the United States. There was also a four-door Chevrolet, a 1940 model, tan in color, which was the "family car." The fourth car, the one used by Mrs. Hummel, was some kind of two-door, the make of which I cannot remember.

On the other side of our Number 21, at Number 19, first lived "Dr." and Mrs. Tierney (he was a foot "doctor" who wore pince-nez glasses), and later on the Goldbergs moved in. This family comprised my mother's friend since school days, Laura Goldberg, her husband "Philly," one of the few dads who was a good athlete, and son Eddie, three years younger than I, who later went to Penn, as I did. Next door were the Decters, Milt and Helen, and their two cute little boys, Phillip and Edward. Then came the Fisher family, who owned Fisher Baking Co., a local company which made Fisher's Buttercup bread, a white bread of the kind typically and unfortunately consumed by most Americans in those years. There was a daughter whom I didn't know very well, whose name may have been Joan, or Carol. Next to the Fishers were the McKim family, headed by Clarence, with whom my dad had gone to high school at either South Side High or Barringer High, both of which my dad attended. The McKims had a daughter, Jane, who was a good softball player (we had an after dinner softball game in the street almost every night in the late spring and summer). Next came the Waltzingers, with two boys, the older boy named Freddy but known as "Snippy," no doubt because he was. I believe that in his adult years he was a banker in Maplewood. After the Waltzingers moved out, in came the Stahls, Marty and his wife Ruth, and two daughters, Judy and Lois. Lois was a rough and ready type who liked sports and who it seems had a crush on me for a while. She married one Sy Fish, a dentist, got divorced, and unfortunately died quite young of cancer. Her sister Judy married a law professor at Rutgers and later on the journalist Milton Viorst. Judy wrote some books reputedly funny, but I never read any of them. I think my wife Greta and sister Rhoda enjoyed them, as did many others. Judy roomed with my cousin Judy Davidson at New Jersey College for Women, later called Douglass College, in their freshman year. Next to the Stahls lived a family named Kneller. I'm pretty sure the father's name was "Cy" or "Sy," and there was a son named Glenn, who was considerably younger than I.

Finally, at the top of the street was a "rich" house whose inhabitants were unknown and never seen. This house had a chimney with some bricks jutting out slightly by an inch or two, for appearance, not by sloppy bricklaying, by means of which my boyhood friend, "super" Bob Olwine would climb to the second story level of the house. Neither I nor anyone else on the street dared to do that. But Bob Olwine did lots of things that no other kid dared do, such as jumping off a tree limb head first with only some kind of rope rig to stop him hitting the ground head first. Bob, incidentally, resided not on Colgate Road but on Salter Place, near Maplewood Junior High, and after fourth grade he moved to the Jefferson School area. We were classmates again later at Maplewood Junior High and at Columbia High.

Across the street, also at the corner of Tuscan Road, was another "rich" house, also with unknown inhabitants. The main reason the residents of the "rich" houses were unknown was, of course, that no kids lived in them. But it must have been more than that, because these people were never ever seen. Next to this was an ordinary house, also with unknown residents. Next came a house very well known to me, that of the Roemmele family, parents Arthur and Gertrude, very fine people, daughter Lois (who became Dean of Admissions at Beaver College, my late wife Greta's *alma mater*), and son Herb, who became my very good friend.

Then came the Nieder family, with a redheaded son, Richard, my age, who was okay but not really a pal. He didn't go to school with us, but to parochial school. Next to the Nieders were the Kroners: Larry and Pearl the parents, Barbara (a year older than I) and Dickey (my sister's worshipful pal). Then, the Kimmels. The paterfamilias was Manuel Kimmel, known as Manny, also known as "Alabama" in the rather unsavory milieu in which he was said to have moved and operated. He was or had been, we were given to understand, some kind of racketeer, gone relatively straight. This may or may not have been accurate, but what is certain is that Mr. Kimmel was a friendly, cheerful man, whom we all liked. When we moved to Colgate Road, neighbors warned my mother never to ride in the Kimmel car, which, of course, was a black Cadillac Fleetwood limousine, lest she risk being shot in a hail of machine gun bullets. There were, in fact, some marks and dents on the doors of this car, and in my imagination these resulted from such a machine gun attack, albeit one that failed to take out the target, Manny Kimmel. Manny's wife was Pauline, who was always quite nice to us, as indeed was Manny. One thing that impressed me inside the Kimmel house was a glass front cabinet which housed an incredible collection of riches in the form of jeweled ivory figures. "That piece cost two thousand dollars," Pauline modestly told my mother, pointing to the largest figure in the case, a king, jewel-encrusted, who may have been Louis XIV. Another Kimmel collection was a dozen or so pairs of men's shoes, all highly polished, which stood on the landing outside the senior Kimmels' bedroom. These I dubbed "Manny's brogues," which my sister thought and still thinks was pretty funny. The Kimmel boys were Seymour and Charley. It seems that Seymour later changed his name to Caesar, which had been his nickname. On reflection, I may be wrong about this. Maybe he *was* originally named Caesar, but I rather doubt it. Caesar was sort of my idol—very good looking, smooth as can be, who joined the U.S. Marine Corps right after high school. Charley, later known as "Chuck," also joined the leathernecks after high school. Charley was a pretty close friend of mine; we spent a lot of time together. He was a great baseball fan, a Dodger fan, and I actually met and had a catch with the magnificent "Pistol Pete" Reiser at the Kimmel house in 1941, the first baseball season I followed, as a true blue new Dodger fan (more about this later).

Caesar's and Charley's lives turned out very differently from those of most of us. Caesar became quite rich, reputedly the third largest shareholder in Warner Communications. Charley opened a series of restaurants in North Jersey. There was one more resident of this unusual Kimmel ménage, Manny "Slim" Polk, Mrs. Kimmel's kid brother. I believe he worked as some sort of "gofer" for big Manny. He used to play in our nightly softball games in the street, all of which ended only when it got too dark to see the ball, after which we went on to "kick the can."

This is as good a point as any to mention another big moment in every late spring and summer evening, the arrival of the Good Humor ice cream truck, driven by a wonderful guy named Mac, who had a thin mustache and who loved kids, and thus his job, too. Popsicles were a nickel, but two specials—burnt almond and coconut Popsicles—were a dime. I think there was also a caramel sundae which may have even cost fifteen cents; I think I actually splurged and had one once.

Back to the neighborhood. Next to the Kimmels were the Pulitos, an Italian family of a certain crudeness and lack of refinement. I remember when Mrs. Pulito's father, or was it her husband, died. That was the first time I ever knew anyone who *DIED*. Well, I didn't really know him, but he lived across the street. The Pulito house was draped in black and purple. Charley Kimmel and I put out our Colgate Road newspaper that day (one of two editions published, printed on some printing press Charley got for Christmas) with a screaming headline "Pulito Dies." There was also a son, Billy, a young adult, who often came home drunk at night, yelling loudly, which caused Mama Pulito to yell back loudly at him. Next to the Pulitos were the Shers, Jack and Golda, with two daughters whose names I can't remember. Wait, one of them was Emily and the other was Barbara. How's that for recall? I used to baby-sit for them at twenty-five cents an hour, or maybe it was fifty. Jack Sher had been a school teacher at South Side High School in Newark (where my mother went, and my dad too for a little while) until he married one of his students, Golda, and went into his father-in-law's leather business. Jack was a very nice guy, much liked by the Colgate Road kids. He actually had a horse and buggy and gave us rides around the neighborhood.

Next to the Shers were, first, the Lewis family, with a daughter named Gail, who was my sister Rho's age. They were succeeded by the Goodmans, daughters Barbara (a year ahead of me) and Muriel ("Mitzi"), in my class at school and a very nice girl. Next to the Goodmans was the Schwartz family, our distant cousins on my mother's side. They were: father Sylvan, mother Sarah, daughters Frankie and Judy, both older than I. Judy was only two years older and was a good pal and a swell gal. Finally there was a son, Lewis, a buddy (or adoring worshipper, more like it) of my sister Rho.

Let's back up a bit. There was another house and family between the Kimmels and Pulitos. This was the Shifman family, father "Sy," with son Bob, several years older than I. I remember one day he was wearing a bright plaid shirt. "Where'd you get that?" I asked. "Arizona," he said, to my amazement. Here was a boy, older but still just a high school guy, who had actually *been* to the Great American West. At that time in my life the farthest west I had been was Philadelphia.

Next to the Schwartzes were the Fasts, with kids Rita, a year older than I, and Mahlon ("Lonny"), Rho's age. Then came the Gonzers with two sons, one much older who went to Cornell, and the other a couple of years older, named Bob, a pleasant fellow. Finally, at the bottom of Colgate next to the vacant lot, lived a Greek-American family named, I think, Sefanides, whom we barely knew.

Since I wrote the above, Herb Roemmele has reminded me that the name of the family that lived in the "rich" house at the top of his side of the street was Pfister and that there was a daughter named Elizabeth, known to the street as Liz, perhaps a year younger than I. Herb also filled in some other lacunae from the Colgate Road geography I spelled out above. There were two houses between his and that of the Pfisters at the top of the street. Next to the Pfisters were the Littels, and then came the Raders. Their children were much older than I, so these families were unknown to me. In the other "rich" house at the top of the street opposite the Pfisters, there lived a crippled boy, who limped up and down the street but associated with none of us Colgate Road kids. Next to that house was that of the Maiers, also quite obscure, who used to complain about our street softball games. Marty Stahl used to complain about them too, especially when a long drive down the left field line broke one of his windows. But since Lois Stahl was a regular in the game, he couldn't complain very harshly. I also had forgotten the Zabarsky (spelling uncertain) family, who lived between the Decters and the Fishers. It was definitely a happy and congenial neighborhood, where everyone knew everyone else.

Henry the mailman. We had the same mailman during all the years that we lived on Colgate Road. His name was Henry, and I can picture him now, carrying his leather bag and moving up our street in long, quick strides, wearing his Post Office-issued gray suit, with black shoes, white shirt and gray or black necktie. He was a refined, well-spoken colored man whom we all liked, with good reason, for he was a fine and likable fellow, "a credit to his race," as one might have condescendingly put it back in those days.

Many readers of these pages will recall that the terms "black" and "African-American" were never used in the 1930s, '40s or '50s. In fact, if you dared to call a colored guy "black" in those days, you might a few seconds later be on your knees searching the ground for your front teeth. I well recall the first time I heard this appellation. It was used by one of my French teachers at the Foreign Service Institute, who referred to "les noirs," i.e., "the blacks." I was both shocked and indeed repelled by these words. Bear in mind that the so-called "n-word" was absolutely forbidden by my parents.

Henry was sincerely interested in the doings of our family, of my sister's and my progression through grade school, junior high, college and (in my case) the Navy. Sadly, however, as those times would have it, we had no such knowledge of him or his family—their last name, where they lived, how many kids he had, where they went to school, etc. Nor should I fail to mention another revealing fact; he and the handful of black kids in our school (in fact, only one or two throughout all my elementary and junior high years) were the *only* colored people we knew at all or talked to other than our maids. For me and for most of us, black people were seen only from the bus or car windows when we drove down Springfield Avenue into Newark, the region "down there," to go to a movie, to a Newark Bears baseball game, or to "Toyland" at Bamberger's department store to see Santa Claus and do Christmas shopping.

Halloween in the Neighborhood. I recall one of my Tuscan School teachers telling us that Halloween meant "hallow evening," falling as it does on October 31, the eve of All Saints Day. However, we kids certainly didn't think of Halloween in terms of saints. We thought of it in terms of candy! And it was indeed an annual event of major importance to us Maplewood children as indeed it was all across the land. It should be recorded at the outset that in those days of the 1930s and 1940s the term "trick or treat" did not exist. We simply walked around the neighborhood in our costumes, rang the doorbells at virtually every house we passed, and were given candies, almost always penny candies, at just about every house.

There were two Halloween-related nights on the two nights preceding the big one. Two nights before was "chalk night," in which we roamed around the neighborhood writing in white chalk on the street and sidewalks. We drew pictures and inscribed supposedly clever (but, I hasten to add, *never* obscene) things on the surfaces. This was followed by "mischief night," in which one thing we did was to ring someone's doorbell and then run away and watch the house's inhabitants answer the door. We usually hid behind bushes as we watched the outcomes of this absolutely original and hilarious prank. The other principal prank was tipping over people's garbage cans. I thought then and think now that these pranks, especially the latter, were not very nice things to do to people from whom we were going to get candy the very next night. Nonetheless I thought nothing of this and participated in mischief night activities. Never mind; that's mild compared with what some kids do these days.

I remember that I more than once dressed as a tramp, an outfit I was partial to for some reason, but one year I was a ghost. That was something of a debacle because I tore my sheet and it rained all night and I was a bedraggled mess.

I think of two other things worthy of note. First, the receptacle we used to put the candy we received into was usually a pillowcase, although large paper bags were also used. Second, there was quite a lovely house at the bottom of the street named the Crescent—a house we thought of as a mansion—where the people who lived therein actually gave out nickel candy bars, such as Baby Ruth and Butterfinger. That was really something in those days. We kids were astonished at how rich those people must have been to demonstrate such remarkable largesse.

Social structures in Maplewood during the 1930s and 1940s. I debated with myself at some length whether to include this section in this memoir. Since you are now reading it, you know the outcome of the debate. My thought is that any description of life in our town in the 1930s and 1940s would be incomplete and therefore not entirely honest without it. Before proceeding, I should set forth three caveats. First, this is written from the standpoint of my own experience of the social mores of the time. Others will of course have experienced them in differing ways; that goes without saying. Second, it is certainly not my intention to offend anyone by what I write here. So, no offense intended and I do hope none will be taken. Third, since I grew up in Maplewood, I shall recall the social structures there and leave most of the discussion of South Orange (the town next to Maplewood whose kids also went to our high school, Columbia) structures to them.

Let's start where the A.E. Newman (i.e., my family) came from, where we lived before moving to Maplewood. Newark, that's where, and that's where many or most Maplewood families lived before making the move west to Maplewood. It's hard to envision now, but Newark actually was a nice city until population migrations, which began at the time of World War I and continued and were intensified in the Depression and World War II years, changed the city's character and composition (yes, I know the euphemisms are coming thick and fast, but I want it that way), probably forever. It's difficult, even impossible, for me to picture Newark making a comeback in the way that certain sections of New York City have done. In any event, Newark neighborhoods were definitely changing, and not for the better, during the Depression years and my parents wanted what all parents everywhere want: a better life for themselves and even more so for their children. So, no doubt screwing up his courage in those economically bad times, my father bought a "Dutch Colonial" house, at number twenty-one Colgate Road in Maplewood for approximately $6,000, of course with the help of a big (relative to the purchase price) mortgage. It was bought from a building and loan company which had foreclosed on it and probably provided the mortgage my dad needed to finance the purchase. How my parents, my sister Rho' and I loved that house, that street, that neighborhood, that town of Maplewood! In my prayers I have always thanked my ancestors for having had the courage and foresight to quit Europe for the bright and happily fulfilled promises of our wonderfully blessed country. ("God looks after drunks, little children, and the United States of America," as one perspicacious observer famously observed). I also thank my parents for having had the foresight to quit Newark for Maplewood, which they did in 1936.

Just as "Gallia est omnia divisa in partes tres," so was the Maplewood of my boyhood. We lived in the middle part, the area bounded by Springfield Avenue and the tracks of the Delaware, Lackawanna and Western Railroad, the two key dividing lines of the town. In this middle section, which was the Tuscan School section, where we lived, and which was itself divided into several sub-sections, families of any religious background could buy and live. In other words, there was not a "gentlemen's agreement" to prevent this in our part of town. But there *was* one in the section above the Lackawanna tracks, known as "The Hill;" this was basically "Protestants only" territory, with a smattering of Catholics. The other section was what we called "The Other Side of Springfield Avenue." This included a smallish sub-section called Vauxhall, which bordered on neighboring Union. This was the least well-off part of town. The Hill was the richest section, while we were in the middle.

In our Tuscan School days we gradually became aware of the social, economic and linguistic distinctions between our part and the other side of Springfield/Vauxhall. We rarely played with kids from that neighborhood. On the Tuscan school playground or at Maplecrest Park, sometimes. In our neighborhood, almost never. In their neighborhood, never. But there were no barriers, religious or otherwise, among the Tuscan kids as a general rule. In fact, we were barely conscious of religion in those early school years. As to race, there was only one colored kid, a very nice girl who was our classmate from first grade through twelfth, in our Tuscan School class. We never thought of her as "colored" or a "Negro," just as a friend and fellow classmate, indeed a well-liked one. Happy, innocent, colorblind days they were back then for us kids. What a pity that couldn't continue.

It was when we left Tuscan School and moved on to Maplewood Junior High that we quickly became more aware of the other two sections of our town, The Hill and The Other Side of Springfield. The latter was definitely considered "down market" when compared with our part of town and another world when compared with the rarified atmosphere of The Hill. We (when I say "we" in this section I refer to myself, my sister and my many good Tuscan pals such as Herb Roemmele, my cousin Joe Carris, Bill Clingan, Dick Martin, *et al*) didn't play with kids from the other side of Springfield. Indeed I even hesitated to set foot over there. Some of the boys there were "tough" and even considered a bit threatening, not to say dangerous. I recall that one day Joe Carris and I deliberately screwed up our courage, got on our bikes and rode over to the Seth Boyden School playground (that section's school) and to DeHart Park (that section's park). To our relief nobody attacked us or even bothered us. In fact, no one paid us the slightest attention, which was in fact something of a letdown.

Maplewood Village. This is the name of the small commercial and shopping center of Maplewood. It is located on Maplewood Avenue, near the DL&W (Delaware, Lackawanna and Western) railroad station, used by Maplewood men who commuted by train to work in New York and Newark. My mother didn't shop in this area simply because it was too long a walk from there to our house (we didn't have a second car then). She shopped in the Springfield Avenue shopping area, described elsewhere in these pages, which was near to our Colgate Road house. Therefore, I didn't get to know "the Village" well until I entered seventh grade at Maplewood Junior High, which was located just near it. The Village was very "up market" compared with the Springfield Avenue area. It served those families who lived on The Hill side of the DL&W tracks.

Now let us take an imaginary walk around the Village. It had a fine old two or three story building which housed the Maplewood public library. This stood in a little park of its own. Unfortunately it no longer survives. It was torn down when the library was moved into a new purpose-built, one story building on the edge of Memorial Park opposite Maplewood Junior High. The Village was the home of various enterprises including: the main office of the Maplewood Bank and Trust Company; the offices of Andrew Jack, Realtor, whose daughter Nancy was in my grade from the seventh grade on; the Maplewood Theater; Parkin's stationery store, Driscoll's food market (a type of store then known as a "grocery" store); Strubbe's ice cream parlor; Foster's drug store; the Rowe 5 & 10 cent store; Leonard's barber shop; and Pietz's delicatessen.

The Pietz family were German immigrants. Their son Ludwig (not exactly a perfect kind of name for an American kid then) was in my grade. He was a good student, but not an athlete. It should be noted that, when considering what kind of guy a boy was, in those days one often could not help but think: athletic or not, good at sports or not. Praise be to the heavens, I was good at sports—not outstanding, but good enough to be a member of both the Eighth Grade Athletic Club and the Ninth Grade Athletic Club. That is why, some sixty years later, I remember that Ludwig Pietz was not an athlete, although he was a whiz in science classes. The athletes were the boys to whom everyone looked up, no doubt about it!

There were three barbers in Leonard's barber shop, all three Italian-Americans. Leonard, the proprietor, who presided over the chair nearest the shop's window, was Italian-born and had a formidable Italian accent. He acted and talked gruff, but was really a very nice man. His passion was the opera. In the shop there was a large floor model radio, probably a Philco. I know this can't be possible but I would swear that every time I went in there for a haircut, the opera was on the radio.

I shall now recount a few things which I remember taking place in the Village. These were really not particularly meaningful or in any way important; they just stuck in my mind for one reason or another. On many a day after school at M.J.H., Joe Carris and I would go to the Village to Pietz's where for a nickel apiece we would buy twelve-ounce bottles of Pepsi Cola. Various classmates, such as Bill Ottey, Clark Benn, Donny Campbell and Dick Witzig, would also turn up there. Then Pepsi spray battles would take place. Here's how we turned our Pepsis into spray weapons. You would put your thumb over the top of the Pepsi bottle and then shake it up vigorously. The carbonation within would then enable you to "shoot" Pepsi spray at your adversaries, by moving your fingers in such a way as to permit a squirt or spray of soda to come shooting out of the head of the bottle.

One day, I was getting a haircut at Leonard's along with some of my classmates. Some of the girls in our class—Jane Raymond, Dorothy Brun and Cynthia Barnes, as I recall—happened by, stopped and looked in at us seated in the barber chairs under barbers' aprons. The girls thought we made an amusing picture. "Look!" shouted one of them, perhaps Dorothy, "Bill Ottey is getting a haircut." Another, probably Jane, said, "Look! Joe Newman is getting one too!" I was very glad to get the attention of these very desirable and attractive girls, to whom I usually found it difficult to talk, so shy was I at that age when it came to girls.

Once I entered Foster's drug store to get myself a five-cent glass of Coca-Cola. There, seated at Foster's soda fountain counter, were Jim Mehorter and Doreen Bradley, real notables from the class ahead of me, i.e., ninth grade. They of course hadn't a clue who I was, but I certainly knew them; everybody did. They were consuming banana splits—*mirabile dictu*!—and Jim was paying for both. What sophistication! And, even more, what incredible wealth! Obviously, Mehorter was very well off indeed; banana splits were twenty-five cents each. Was I impressed by this? You know it; do I not remember it distinctly more than sixty years later?

Local Stores. In that wonderful age before the coming of supermarkets and other mega stores, people did their shopping right in their own neighborhoods, at little stores owned by small merchants whom one knew personally and with whom one chatted while making purchases. Of course in those days very few mothers had their own cars, so they simply walked to these neighborhood stores. I can still visualize many of these stores quite well. The local grocery store which my mother patronized most was Freda's, owned by a gigantic German immigrant named Freda Korn, who had a friendly, ne'er-do-well husband named Tony, who sometimes hung about the store and helped Freda. Freda was a most affable woman, about whom my grandfather, Dr. Joe Kussy, composed the following ditty:

> "I know my heart.
> I know my mind.
> I know that Freda
> Sticks out behind."

Food stores then had shelves which reached up to or almost up to the ceiling. The storekeepers used poles with a kind of pincer on the end to reach merchandise on the upper shelves. To set the geography, Freda's store was located on the southwest corner of Springfield Avenue and Wellesley Street. Next door to Freda's was Matter's drug store, owned by the Matter brothers. This had the then traditional red and green globes in the window. Bob Matter was a rather dour individual, whereas his brother Charley, short and rotund (Bob was taller and quite thin), was quite jovial. Come to think of it, they were something of a Mutt and Jeff team. I didn't go there often, because they didn't carry candy—at least not the kind we kids liked, but only the boxes of candy which people used to give and still do, I believe, as gifts. In those days drug stores were primarily pharmacies, with a smattering of other products.

Next to Matter's was the Maplecrest Hardware. I used to go in there from time to time. The proprietor was exactly the type you would expect to own a hardware store—stocky, partly bald and always chewing on a cigar.

Next to Maplecrest Hardware was a vacant lot, on which a U.S. Post Office was eventually built, after which came a small one-story brick building housing Roland's barber shop. It had the traditional red and white barber's pole outside, as indeed did virtually all barber shops in those days. Roland was a somewhat portly chap, quite pleasant, who knew and cut the hair of just about every boy in our neighborhood. If I remember correctly, haircuts were then fifty or sixty cents.

Farther to the west on the south side of Springfield Avenue, at the southwest corner of that avenue and Rutgers Street, was a two or three story building with three little stores, the middle one of which was Abe's, owned and operated by Abe Greenberg and his wife. How can I describe this kind of store, which was very common then but hardly exists anymore? They were generally known as "luncheonettes" or "candy stores." I can best convey an image of what they were like by telling what they sold: cigars, cigarettes, pipes and pipe tobacco, comic books, magazines, candy (one, five and ten cent varieties), stationery items. There was also a "lending library," very rare now, if indeed they still exist at all. For a nickel a day, one could borrow the latest novels. My mother, a great reader of novels, made good use of this feature. There was also a soda fountain, where you could get simple sandwiches, Coca-Cola, fruit flavored sodas (fruit syrup plus seltzer) and ice cream sodas. "Black and white" sodas (chocolate soda with vanilla ice cream) were my favorite; Mom favored "all black."

Comic books and candy. Abe's store was my main source of two very important boyhood items—comic books and candy.

As you entered the store, displayed magnificently on the left were racks bearing a wonderful plethora of magazines of all kinds and scores of comic books, also known as funny books. During my later Tuscan School days, when my "allowance" was fifty cents a week, I would regularly repair to Abe's after school on Fridays and judiciously spend three-fifths of my weekly stipend for the purchase of three comic books. The selection was wide so it was necessary to browse at some length through many comics in order to select the week's trio. It is an absolute fact that comic books then contained sixty-four pages, a number which over the years was gradually reduced to thirty-two pages even as their price rose from ten cents to a quarter and on up. In their early days, the super heroes appeared with other stories. Thus Superman was found in Action Comics; Batman and Robin (my own personal favorites among all the super heroes) in Detective Comics. Superman was invulnerable to bullets and could fly. Batman and Robin were regular human beings, Bruce Wayne and Dick Grayson, and though not invulnerable they managed always to evade any and all bullets fired at them.

Another great hero was Captain Marvel. He was in fact a newsboy named Billy Batson who when he uttered the magical incantation "SHAZAM" transformed into Captain Marvel. Aficionados of this particular super hero will of course recall that he first appeared in Whiz Comics in February 1940 and that SHAZAM was an acronym standing for:

Solomon (wisdom)
Hercules (strength)
Atlas (stamina)
Zeus (power)
Achilles (courage)
Mercury (speed)

Another super hero was the Human Torch, a man who by simply willing it turned into a man-shaped flame. He would throw little fireballs at the bad guys in the process of subduing them. He had an arch-enemy called the Submariner, a bad guy with pointed ears who lived in the briny deep. The Submariner quickly became such a popular figure that his creator was obliged to turn him into a good guy, a crime fighting ally of the Human Torch. Other costumed heroes were the Phantom, the Green Lantern and the Fox. There were a number of others, but their names and appearances now escape me.

As I got older I began to buy and read other monthly publications. I regularly read several "pulp" magazines of baseball stories, the Sporting News, Baseball Digest, Street and Smith's annual surveys of all the big league baseball teams and of football teams, both pro and college, and "Doc Savage." It must be that at some point my father increased my allowance, thus enabling me to widen my reading horizons. My mom and dad were never concerned about the quality of my reading matter. They believed that being a reader was the important thing. If I read comic books and baseball stories and stuff like Doc Savage as a boy, as

I became older my horizons would widen and I would develop into a reader of a wide variety of good books, both fiction and nonfiction. They were right; that's exactly what happened. If I had to make an estimate of how many books I have read since entering junior high school, I would say that by now, at age seventy-five, I have over the years read some two thousand books. And if I am fortunate enough to live long enough to do so, I hope to read another six or seven hundred.

As to Abe's candy counter, what a profusion of delicious treats! On the right side of Abe's, in front of the cigar and cigarette counter, were displayed a wide variety of nickel candy bars, including Baby Ruth, Butterfinger, O'Henry, Jujyfruits, Jujubes, Peanut Chews, Milk Duds, Hershey bars, Nestle bars, Suchard bars, Mounds and Almond Joys (these two were ten cents each), Whiz, Necco Wafers, Dots, Black Crows, Good and Plenty, Turkish Taffy, Chuckles, Mars, Snickers, Three Musketeers, Forever Yours, Milky Way, Bit-O-Honey and Walnettos. I liked all of these except Necco Wafers, Black Crows and Good and Plenty (I disliked licorice then, and still do).

On the left side of the store was a display case with sliding glass doors containing penny candies, which for some reason were known in our family as "pawnies," a name made up by my grandfather, Dr. Joe Kussy, who almost always had a little paper bag full of pawnies in his coat pocket (and he a dental surgeon!). Obviously the word was derived from "pennies," which was what these delicious candies cost. My favorites were chocolate "twists," Tootsie Rolls, candy bananas, root beer barrels, and malted milk balls. I wish I had a little bag of pawnies on my desk right now!

At the back of the store on the right was the soda fountain. Here one could get small and large Cokes (a nickel and a dime), small cherry or lemon sodas (three cents), egg salad and tuna salad sandwiches (fifteen or twenty cents, I think, or possibly a quarter). Thus one could get a light lunch at a price of twenty to thirty-five cents. Isn't it incredible what government has done to our money in the intervening years?

A digression. A few doors down Rutgers Street from the corner building in which Abe's was located lived a girl who was a "Mongolian idiot." What an awful name; such unfortunates are called Down Syndrome people today, but the former term was the one in use during my boyhood days. In any event, the first time I saw this poor girl and heard her speak, I was very, very upset. It scared me. How could any kid be like that? Every time I went to Abe's I was in fear that I would see her, because she walked up to Abe's from time to time.

Moving west on the south side of Springfield Avenue for a couple of streets, one came to Mangieri's, an "ice cream parlor." Then in a building on the southwest corner of Springfield Avenue and Prospect Street, there was Topf's Pharmacy, which we patronized more than we did Matter's, and Sweet's delicatessen. The latter was utilized often, especially on Sundays, when "the bunch" (as my mother called them) came to 21 Colgate Road for a late afternoon/early evening visit. On those days, supper for the bunch (who were in fact my father's family, discussed elsewhere in these pages) was invariably "cold cuts," an oft-used term in those days but much less so today. I still use the term, and whenever daughter Jessie hears me do so, she kids me greatly about it.

Farther down the south side of Springfield Avenue in this block was Kahn's dry goods store, where Mom took me each year in late August for "back to school" clothes.

Now let's cross to the north side of Springfield Avenue. Opposite Topf's Pharmacy was the Crestmont Savings and Loan, located on the northwest corner of Springfield Avenue and Prospect Street (pals Myron "Midge" Glickfeld and Danny Mishell lived a few doors down Prospect Street, at numbers 728 and 730 respectively). One lot in from the northeast corner was the Maplewood Bank and Trust Company, where I had my first ever checking account. The manager was a Mr. Seymour, who to me looked like what I always visualized Casper Milquetoast as looking like. Then came (heading east) another barber shop which I often went to, even though I preferred Roland's (it may be that I started going to Roland's later). I think my father preferred this one, but I certainly did not. There were always men there, whereas Roland's was mostly for kids, and the barbers were, in my eyes, sourpusses, especially the owner, who Dad insisted be the one to cut my hair. I have forgotten his name, but I can still see in my mind's eye the name of the make of the barber chair, emblazoned on the footrest part of the chair: Emil J. Paidar, Chicago, Illinois. I once overheard this owner tell a customer, or those present in general: "Over there, they're fighting for their lives. Over here they're fighting for the money." (This was during the Second World War). This greatly disturbed the innocent boy I then was. Before we leave the subject of barber shops, I should record that it was later during my years at Maplewood Junior High that I preferred to have my hair cut at Leonard's in Maplewood Village, as mentioned before, a most congenial establishment.

At the northwest corner of Springfield Avenue and Rutgers Street there was an Esso station where we bought our gasoline. I remember the gas pump jockey there—not the owner, an employee—once telling my mother that he made $70 a week at his job. "Could you live on that?" he asked my mother. I can't recall her reply. On the northeast corner was a very important place, the White Castle. Their hamburgers ("Buy 'em by the sack!" was their motto) cost five cents, and I consumed hundreds of them. On school days when Mom and Aunt Sylvia (Joe Carris's mother, my mother's older sister) were out together, e.g., shopping at Bamberger's in Newark, Joe Carris and I, who had lunch together virtually every day from the first grade through sixth grade, alternating between the Carris house and ours, would eat at the White Castle and then go back to Tuscan School for the afternoon session. My mother would give me fifteen cents for this lunch—two hamburgers and a chocolate milk. As I recall, it was always the same person, a very pleasant and cheerful woman named Helen, who had false teeth, who served them up to us.

Farther east on Springfield Avenue, on the northeast corner of Springfield and Wellesley Street, was a diner. I believe it had several owners and names over the years, but the one I remember best was "Ben's." I patronized this place too. In addition to good hamburgers, in fact better than the White Castle's and costing a dime, they had delicious doughnuts. Moving further east, a pedestrian would come upon Denk's grocery store, owned and operated by the Denk brothers, a somewhat austere pair. Mom shopped there as well as at Freda's. Next to Denk's was a Sunoco station, after which came Maplecrest Park.

Wait, let's back up a bit. I forgot Kleest's ice cream parlor, located on the north side of Springfield Avenue, in the block between the Maplewood Bank and Trust and the Esso station. We went to Kleest's often, in fact more than to Mangieri's. In later years, though, particularly after I started at Columbia High School, we went often to the famous Gruning's ice cream parlor in South Orange center, a very busy place. Kleest's was a very quiet place, never more than a few customers. But it was nearby, so we would walk there frequently. Mom loved their sodas, and Mangieri's too.

On Springfield Avenue opposite Maplecrest Park there was a cluster of small stores, including a little dry cleaning and tailor shop operated by a little Armenian man of indeterminate (to me at any rate) age. Our family did not have our dry cleaning done there as we patronized Mrs. Ross's Hand Laundry, which also did dry cleaning and offered the valuable service of pick-up and delivery (important because my mother didn't have a car of her own until 1947 when in the flush of post-war prosperity my dad bought her an Oldsmobile two-door "coupe"). What business Mom did give to the Armenian consisted of small tailoring jobs now and then. Eventually this led him to express the following plaint to my mother in his interestingly accented and high-pitched English: "Mrs. Newman, I can't make any money on you."

Farther east, on a street running diagonally south off Springfield Avenue, was Mutter and Coryell, the bicycle store, where we took our bikes when they needed repairs. During all my school years, I had only two bicycles, both Iver Johnsons, the first a "24," the second a "28." Mr. Mutter was the father of my friend Ray Mutter, a swell boy. When the Mutters moved to Chatham, after seventh grade, this bike shop became just plain "Ray Coryell."

Maplecrest Park. I spent many a morning, afternoon and early evening at nearby Maplecrest Park, especially on summer vacation days and mostly during my years at Tuscan School (after I started at Maplewood Junior High, I went more often to Memorial Park, located opposite that school). Joe Carris almost invariably went with me to the park, or met me there. In the autumn, it was to play football. For a couple of years we had a team called the Martin Maulers (Dick Martin was our captain). In spring and summer it was to play baseball, the "summer game," my favorite then, now and always. There were three ball fields at Maplecrest and we played on the one that was available on any given day. In addition to playing, we also watched the "big guys" (high school boys) play, hoping that some day we would be able to play as well as they did.

There was a pond area, a depression in the ground, man-made I am sure, which was flooded every winter for ice skating. This we did in the afternoon or early evening on winter days when the pond was frozen solid. I have a good recollection of the "shelter house," where we changed into our skates before skating and out of them afterwards. There was always a most welcome, warming fire in a large fireplace. The shelter house also had ping pong tables, at which Joe and I played many a game. We also played tennis at the park, where there were a few good clay courts. Although we were in those days quite equally matched, Joe left me behind in the sport as years passed, and eventually he became a varsity player at Columbia High School.

The Fourth of July. Maplewood always had a full and excellent program held each year at Memorial Park, to celebrate Independence Day. We never missed this event during all the years we lived in Maplewood. There were four parts to the program; a nominally priced red, white and blue ticket gained one admission to all four.

The day began with a morning track meet, consisting primarily of foot races. Kids from all grades from first to ninth participated in these. Although I was a pretty fast runner, I never did manage to come in first in a race; perhaps I came in second or third a couple of times. The winner in our grade was almost always Milward ("Dick") Martin, of Oakview Avenue, the fastest and tallest boy in our grade, who went on to varsity basketball and swimming and track at Columbia High School.

In the afternoon there was a circus, which we kids of course enjoyed a lot. Then at dusk families gathered on the park lawn opposite the town hall and enjoyed a band concert, awaiting the denouement of the day's program, the fireworks. We kids would be squirming with anticipation during the concert, eagerly awaiting the onset of darkness so the big show could begin. Then suddenly—bang, whoosh, boom!—the first rocket would shoot up into the night sky and explode in that ever so thrilling burst of colors. How we loved it! The fireworks display always ended with many rockets being fired simultaneously, lighting up the night with a veritable fountain of noise and light. It was quite thrilling to one and all, both young and old, and it was the perfect ending to the day of classic Americana. I can still remember how very happy and fine we felt walking home after the show, and how fortunate and proud we were to be citizens of our wonderful country.

.

SCHOOL DAYS

My Teachers: A Special Memory

Tuscan School

Special Events

Maplewood Junior High

Columbia High School

My teachers—A special memory. I'm deeply grateful to the generally good to excellent teachers of the Maplewood schools I attended: Tuscan, Maplewood Junior High and Columbia High. From kindergarten to high school graduation my fellow students and I were fortunate enough to be guided by a quite special group of teachers who did more than just teach us. They instilled positive values, motivated and inspired us to work hard and succeed.

My first grade teacher at Tuscan was Miss Hart whom, no doubt because I was then only six years old, I don't remember well. But in second grade I had a teacher whom I can remember as a distinct personality. This was Miss O'Neill, a young and perky woman of Irish background who was possessed of a pleasing manner. She became Mrs. Carrigan not long after my year in her class, which was 1938-39.

My third grade class was presided over by the formidable if somewhat eccentric Miss Sinon, a good teacher. I clearly recall one aspect of learning about which she was an absolute stickler—the multiplication tables. To drum them into our little minds absolutely and forever she used the tool of "flash cards." These had numbers and a notation, e.g., 7 x 9, on the side she would show us and the answer, 63, on the reverse side. The class would sit in a semi-circle around her and she would "flash" the cards at one after the other of us in sequence and we would recite the correct answer. Did this method work? Yes, perfectly and permanently for most of us.

In fourth grade I had a first-class teacher whom we were very fond of, Miss Cox, who shortly after my year in her class became Mrs. Randolph. Then, in fifth grade, there was the delightful Miss Mildred Hettger, who generally wore a smock and often brown and white shoes. What a swell teacher she was! She was deservedly famous for bestowing upon Joe Carris, Herb Roemmele and me the exalted title of the "Purple Trio". Of all the fine teachers I was privileged to have, she is the one I would most like to locate and talk to now. Indeed, once in the early 1990s, I wrote a letter to the Maplewood Board of Education identifying myself as a former pupil of hers and asking if they could provide her address. Unfortunately they could not, but they did inform me she had retired in the mid or late 1960s.

In the sixth grade, my last year at Tuscan, from which I graduated in 1943, my teacher was the excellent Miss Cooper, older than the other teachers at Tuscan, gray-haired, somewhat fragile in speech—she spoke very quietly—and manner. She was not the kind of teacher we kids loved in the way we loved Miss Hettger, but we certainly did respect her.

The reader will note that all of my elementary school teachers were women. The reason is simple; there were no men teachers in the Maplewood elementary schools. We first had men teachers at Maplewood Junior High. I'll now write about some of the teachers I had at that fine school, which I entered in September 1943.

Maplewood Junior High. First and foremost, I think of the wonderful Miss Ferguson, my math teacher in both the seventh and eighth grades, universally known as "Ma," but of course never to her face. She was a lively and delightful middle-aged woman who taught her subject well. As a result, I learned it well. It was one of my favorite subjects, one in which I received good "marks," as grades were then called.

This is an appropriate point at which to describe the report cards that we received monthly throughout our twelve years of pre-college schooling. In the "grade" (i.e., elementary) schools, i.e., grades one through six, the reports were in commentary form, e.g., "Joseph works well with others," or as Miss Hart once famously—in my family—wrote: "Joseph is apt to run around the room." In junior high, grades seven to nine, we received letter grades with numerical notations, e.g., A-1, the number one indicating, if memory serves, "attentive, active, interested in work." Finally at Columbia High we received numerical grades such as 85, 88 and 90. The highest such I ever got was a 95 in Algebra II, a subject I loved. The lowest was an 80 in Latin II, which I detested and which was absolutely my worst subject. In fact I did so badly and this was so out of character for me that my Latin teacher, Miss Caswell, called or wrote to my mother asking if I was having any problems at home. I was not, as she easily could have and should have known had she bothered to look at how I was doing in my other subjects, in which I was averaging about 90. Latin was my only bad subject, which must have disappointed Miss Caswell because I had taken Latin in the eighth and ninth grades and received sixteen consecutive A's in sixteen "marking periods." It was all my own fault; she was not a bad teacher.

I note that, in this discussion of the grading methods, I have somehow jumped ahead to high school without completing my recollections of Maplewood Junior High teachers. So, now back to the MJH teaching staff. There was Miss Clark, who taught "social studies" (whatever that was); Miss Cunnison, who taught science and was easily the oldest teacher in that school; the McAdam (MacAdam?) sisters, both of whom taught English and were austere and strict spinsters; Mr. Dennis Morris, who taught Algebra I and also served as the coach of the Eighth Grade Athletic Club; Mrs. Short, who taught Latin when

I was good at it; the young and lovely Miss Harylw (pronounced "Harillyou"), who was just starting her teaching career and whom I adored; Mrs. Hellstrom, a highly attractive woman who taught reading; Miss Wallace, who taught us world history; Mr. John Morgan, who taught American history; and Miss Cain, another English teacher. The school principal was Mr. Ross Runnels, an austere and redoubtable figure who administered the school from his lofty height with virtually no personal contact with its students except for occasional appearances at Friday "assemblies," i.e., the weekly gathering of the entire student body in the school auditorium. Finally, and to me importantly, there was Mr. John Tice, the "phys ed" teacher referred to elsewhere in these pages as the coach of the Ninth Grade Athletic Club.

Columbia High School. A glance at the 1949 "Mirror" (or any other Mirror for that epoch), our class yearbook, which I edited in my senior year with the able assistance of Bob Morris, Sue Conkling, Bob Mielich and others, will reveal the names and subjects of the entire faculty of Columbia High in those post-war years. The list is a long one—there were close to 1,500 kids from Maplewood and South Orange at Columbia—so I won't attempt an extensive listing of their names. Instead I'll recall some who stand out in my memory. The principal was Mr. Frederick Crehan, the vice-principal Mr. Johnson. A great favorite was Miss Mildred Memory, a delightful woman who taught American history and never gave us any homework assignments—the *only* teacher who did not do so; Mr. Mellotte, geometry; Mr. Perry Tyson, who taught Algebra II and was an assistant football coach. The other "phys ed" teachers were Mr. Roy Nuttall, the head coach of the basketball and baseball teams; Mr. Philip Seitzer, the track coach; and Mr. Hoffman, the head football coach. Finally, I'll list the above-mentioned Miss Caswell; the excellent Miss Ruth Paine, who taught me English in my senior year and who was kind enough to write in my yearbook: "To Joe, a man of *belles lettres*;" Mr. Wenker, my homeroom teacher for three years and faculty advisor to the Mirror staff; and the delightful Mrs. Ahern, one of my absolute favorites, who taught Spanish.

I sadly realize that many, perhaps the majority, or all these fine teachers of my school years are no longer of this world. Wherever they are, I now thank and express my appreciation to them. Would that men and women of their high caliber staffed America's public schools today.

Tuscan School. In the summer of 1937 we moved from our rented house at Boyden Avenue, Maplewood to our recently built and newly purchased house at 21 Colgate Road, the house of my childhood, boyhood and school years. In September, I started out in the first grade at Tuscan School, a very good and attractive school, located on a lovely site between Harvard Avenue and Tuscan

Road, below Prospect Street and above Valley Street. The site had a nice little brook, complete with waterfall and bridge.

I remember that in first grade my teacher was Miss Hart. Cousin Joe Carris (he's actually Sol Joseph Carris) was not in my class (however, we were together in the same class, along with Herb Roemmele, from second through sixth grades). Joe and Herb were next door, in Miss Marden's class. I remember one little incident. Early in the school year, a little blonde-haired boy was brought into our class, and was introduced to us by Miss Hart as the boy from Miss Marden's class who was doing so wonderfully well at everything in the first grade work. The little angel—you could almost see the golden halo above his golden hair—was, I am certain of it, holding a school book and a pencil as he quietly accepted the accolades heaped upon him by Miss Hart. Not long afterward I learned that this little boy was none other than Herbert Arthur Roemmele, who lived up the street from us at 10 Colgate Road, and with whom I soon became good friends, a friendship which has now lasted almost seventy years.

Some of the other kids in my grades through the six wonderful Tuscan years were Ilene Abramson, Barbara Alpaugh, Jack Bain, Vern Beaney, Dean Behrend, Michael Christie (who moved away along about fifth grade), Bill Clingan, Barbara Evans, Myron ("Midge") Glickfeld, Muriel ("Mitzi") Goodman, Emily Grady (the class beauty), Claire Hummel, Bob Lanes, Helen Leister, Joan Litzbauer, Bob Maglie, Milward ("Dick") Martin, Constantine ("Connie") Maskaleris, Patsy Meeker, Helen Metheny (who moved away early on), Bob Moore, Ray Mutter, Bob Olwine, Rita Rado, Walter ("Pete") Rauscher, Ken Robson, Pete Rommel, Jean Russell, Don ("Max") Satterfield, Frank Schoner, Anne Slater (the best girl athlete), Dick Somers, Jean Szeremany, Carole Taylor, Joanne Volz, Eddie Wallace, Mary Lou Wester, and Bob Woodnorth.

Hark back to the teachers. I forgot to mention Miss Ireland, the principal, and Miss McQuilken, the janitress.

After setting down the above list of Tuscan kids, I went over it with Joe Carris and between the two of us we came up with quite a few more names, as follows: Ann ("Babs") Wilson, Quane ("Tex") Risinger, Robert Ernie, Danny Mishell, Ray Burkhardt, Sam Farinella, Nancy Lafler, Norman Thomas, Marilyn Hankins, Bob Bolster, John Harrity, Walter Leonard, Nancy Seitel, Don Lawshe, Tom Buonassissi (spelling very uncertain), Bill Evans, Bernie Edelman, Aaron Goode, Ann Robinson, Jim Shotwell, Freddie Kuchen, Bob Padalino, Joan Willitts, and Barbara Hendricks. Three other names come to mind, kids who may have gone to Tuscan but possibly went to other grade schools in Maplewood: Barbara Betts, Ruth Flegenheimer and Virginia Thiele.

Let me recount some memories that have stuck in my mind about some of the above schoolmates.

Ilene Abramson. She lived on the next street, Rutgers Street, and was a very nice, attractive girl, friendly and a good pal. Still attractive at our fiftieth reunion.

Barbara Alpaugh. She lived near Joe Carris and participated in various outdoor games we used to play in his neighborhood.

Jack Bain. A very skinny little guy, but smart. He sat in front of me in Miss Cooper's sixth grade class. He grew up to become a successful lawyer in North Jersey, and active in the Republican Party.

Vern Beaney. He was a good guy, who came to my house more than a few times. Unfortunately, he died relatively young.

Dean Behrend. A close pal for a few years, he lived across the street from Joe Carris. When he turned up at our Tuscan School fiftieth reunion in Maplewood in 1993, he was totally unrecognizable. This isn't to say that he didn't look good because he did. Afterwards, Joe Carris and I used to say: "Who do you suppose that guy was who said he was Dean Behrend?"

Michael Christie. A rough and ready guy, who lived opposite Dick Martin on Oakview Avenue. He moved away about the time we were in sixth or seventh grade. I was sorry he left.

Bill Clingan. Another rough and ready guy, who lived on Harvard Avenue. I used to call for him at his house on the way to school. He was a very good pal of mine, so we walked to school together most days. His mother, a delightful lady, would often give me a bowl of oatmeal topped with brown sugar on days when I called for him. It was delicious. Bill joined the Marines after attending Purdue University. As a Marine, in what he called "a moment of madness," he got a tattoo. Then I didn't see him for almost thirty years, when I sought him out and found him living in the San Francisco Bay area. I was glad to see him.

Barbara Evans. She was a swell girl, a tomboy, whose company I much enjoyed. A good pal.

Myron Glickfeld. "Midge" was what was in those days called a "wild" kid. We were quite friendly during high school years.

Emily Grady. She was our Tuscan School beauty, as nice as she was pretty.

Bob Lanes. Another rough and ready, very likable guy. I played with him often over the years. He was very friendly with Midge Glickfeld, near whom he lived. Bob, who married Kathy Bolan, also in our high school class, came to all our school reunions. Once he had the chance to buy an old car, something like a Maxwell, for $50. I was dying to buy it with him on a 50-50 basis, so I asked my dad's permission, explaining to him what a fantastic bargain it was at $50. Permission refused. Reason: "And who is going to pay for the repairs?"

Joan Litzbauer. She was a very nice girl, whom I often met on the way to school because our routes met on Harvard Avenue. Joan has remained in

Maplewood and comes to *every* reunion—Tuscan, MJH and Columbia—at which she is always good company and well liked by one and all.

Bob Maglie. He was a rough and ready guy from the "down market" end of Maplewood, i.e., near Springfield Avenue up at the Vauxhall neighborhood. He was a regular player in our very frequent after school (Tuscan) football and baseball games at Maplecrest Park. In fact he was the quarterback on the Martin Maulers football team.

Milward ("Dick") Martin. Dick lived on Oakview Avenue, not far from Joe Carris. He was the tallest boy in our class from early Tuscan years right through high school. Dick was a very nice, friendly lad who was a good athlete with a tremendous size advantage. Naturally he played first base in baseball and center in basketball. In addition, he was an outstanding swimmer, quite possibly all-state. As the name implies, he was captain of the Martin Maulers in Tuscan days, playing fullback.

Connie Maskaleris. A friendly, always smiling boy of you'll never guess what national origin! Unfortunately, he died a few years ago.

Helen Metheny. She was one of the two class beauties, the blonde one (the brunette one was Emily Grady). She moved away from Maplewood early on during Tuscan years. Shockingly, indeed almost unbelievably, her older sister died while we were at Tuscan, perhaps in second grade. It was the first time we were confronted at first hand with the highly disturbing reality that children could die.

Ray Mutter. Ray was a pleasant and well-liked boy. As mentioned, his father was half owner of the bicycle shop, Mutter and Coryell, where we took our bikes for repairs. Unfortunately, after seventh grade, he moved to Chatham.

Bob Olwine. Bob was one of my early good school friends. He was a remarkable boy who in addition to being very likable was the most acrobatic of any of the kids at our school. After fourth grade, he moved to the Jefferson School area. I was very sorry to see him leave, but of course we became classmates again in seventh grade and remained so throughout junior high school and high school. My most vivid memory of Bob as an acrobat was his climbing the chimney at the "rich house" at the top of Colgate Road, as mentioned earlier. Bob used the brick protrusions on the chimney as footholds and handholds and climbed the chimney to the second story level, where there was a setback which provided a place to stand. I was absolutely awed by this—no other kid dared to do this, ever—and immediately proclaimed that Bob was "super." He affected diffidence about this appellation, but I know that he really liked it very much.

He performed another incredible feat of skill and bravery when we were in seventh grade. One day after school when other boys and I went up to his house to play, Bob gave us an amazing demonstration. He had fixed a strong rope to a stout branch of a tree in his backyard. At the end of the rope was a board about an inch thick and perhaps six inches wide and four feet long. Bob put the board just behind his rear end, with the rope coming out front through his legs. Then, legs pressed tightly together, he jumped backwards off the limb. The rope and board stopped his fall, with a big bounce, when his head was twelve to eighteen inches from the ground. Now *that* was something really super! (The term "super" was of course derived from our comic book hero, Superman). Nobody else ever dared attempt this remarkable feat, not even Clark ("Muscles") Benn. We all just stood there agape, knowing we were in the presence of a boy of utmost skill and bravery.

At our fortieth Columbia High School reunion, held at the Hotel Suburban in Summit, I saw Bob again for the first time in forty years (I may have seen him during college years, but I don't think I did). He was now significantly taller and as handsome as ever, indeed more so judging from our female classmates' reaction to him. A thoracic surgeon, he had recently moved back east, to the Eastern Shore of Maryland, after many years in the State of Washington. This great friendship, restored after an interruption of so many years, has continued to the present day, and I am sure, will continue to flourish in the years ahead.

Jean Russell. Jean was a swell girl, liked by one and all, who lived in a big old wooden house on Tuscan Road, just a few streets away from our house on Colgate Road. My main recollection of her is of a day when, walking home from Tuscan after school, I came upon her bouncing a rubber ball on the sidewalk in front of her house and stopped for a few minutes to talk. My memory is of a pretty and friendly girl in a neat dress and with long, brown straight hair. Jean became an actress and, although never well-known as such, was not unsuccessful in her career. And she remained nice. At our fiftieth Tuscan School reunion, organized by Herb Roemmele and me, our classmate Rita Rado recounted how she had run across Jean playing in a summer theater somewhere out west, had talked with her and found her as delightful and friendly as ever. We were most happy to hear this. Unfortunately, Rita's tale was told against the sad background fact of Jean's death a few years before.

Jean Szeremany. Jean was very good at school, very actively engaged in school activities of various kinds, very neat, very well groomed and with perfect deportment at all times.

Eddie Wallace. I was quite friendly with Eddie for a few years. He was a great baseball enthusiast like myself. There were a couple of summers, probably after sixth and fifth grade, and maybe after seventh too, when a bunch of us boys played baseball at Memorial Park every morning and afternoon. Well, *almost* every day. Eddie was a catcher in those games.

Quane ("Tex") Risinger. As his nickname implies, Quane and his family moved to Maplewood from Texas. He was a good guy and a good baseball player (he was a catcher), good at football too.

Robert Ernie. This boy's father worked for Cities Service Oil Co. How do I know this? Because one fine day at Tuscan, Robert gave every boy and girl in our class a pen with the words "Cities Service Oil Co." on it, and a blob of oil, under glass, in the handle of the pen.

Danny Mishell. Another interesting boy. He was a very good student who seemed always to be a step ahead of the rest of us in our reading assignments at school. After a few years, Dan moved with his family to San Francisco where his father, a U.S. Army doctor, was assigned. Dan and I were good friends. I was sorry when he left.

Ray Burkhardt. Ray was the shortest boy in our grade at Tuscan, consistently from year to year. The Burkhardts must have been a rather poor family, because they lived in a house that was little more than a shack, located on Springfield Avenue, up near the Vauxhall section, where all the Italian immigrant boys lived. The Burkhardt house was a source of both amazement and a kind of horror to me. It was difficult for me to believe that a boy at Tuscan School was so poor.

Similarly, later during a Maplewood Junior High School year, I one day walked home with Murdock Merchant, a swell guy who sadly is no longer with us, perhaps the best athlete, or certainly one of the best, in the school. We came to a building on Valley Street, one with stores on the ground floor. To my astonishment, Murdock said goodbye and mounted a staircase to the "flat above a store" in which he lived with his family. I could hardly believe it; Murd actually lived above a store. How could anyone in Maplewood be so poor, I wondered.

Sam Farinella. Sammy was one of those Italian immigrants (perhaps he was born in the USA, but his parents certainly were not) who lived in the Vauxhall section. He had an older brother, Joe. These "Italians" fascinated me. Jim Puglio and Bob Padalino were others in this Italian group. There were very rough looking and acting guys, quite different from the likes of Joe Carris, Herb Roemmele, Bob Olwine and Bill Clingan!

"Spring, spring, my name is Ming." In the spring of 1940, when I was in Miss Sinon's third grade class, that worthy teacher gave our class a nice assignment, to write a poem about spring. The one I composed went as follows:

> Spring, spring, my name is Ming.
> With birds always on the wing.
> In spring, I like to look at pines,
> And whiz! I find a dime
> And buy a lime fizz.
> And for supper I had a pea.

A few explanatory comments are in order. Ming was a Fu Manchu-like villain who was pitted against Flash Gordon (one of my comic book and strip heroes) in a story episode entitled, as I recall, "The Moons of Mongo." No doubt this episode was current at the time I composed my poem. As to "birds on the wing," that may have come from my grandfather Joe Kussy's poem which went:

> The poets write concoining spring
> And say the boid is on the wing.
> But 'pon my woid
> 'Tis most absoid.
> Is not the wing upon the boid?

A lime fizz of course was a popular drink in those days. As for the last line, it quite puzzles me. Although I was hardly a hearty eater at that age, it's difficult to think of my being satisfied with a supper consisting of one pea!

There is an interesting footnote which must be recorded here. I myself had absolutely no memory of my "Spring . . . Ming" poem as an adult. It slipped back into my unconscious mind not long after I wrote it. But for some reason my third grade classmate, Bob Olwine, was impressed by my opus and memorized it. Not only that; for years he used to recite it at Olwine family occasions! I only learned of this when I "found" Bob again at the aforementioned fortieth Columbia High School reunion. After that event Bob told me about my poem and recited it to me.

Families rarely moved. Because families seldom moved during the 1930s and the war years, only rarely did new kids arrive at Tuscan School, or old regulars move away. I can think of a couple of new boys during Tuscan school years. One was Don Satterfield. He arrived during the middle of the school year, I think in our sixth and final grade school year, when our teacher was Miss Cooper. On the day Don first came to school, the teacher announced that we were to welcome a new student, Don Satterfield, to our class. After school, Herb Roemmele, who was also in Miss Cooper's class, asked me: "What's the new guy's name?" I hadn't listened very well either, so I replied, "Oh, I don't know, something like Max Sakowski." Poor Don. Max became his nickname from that moment forward, and it endured at least through high school. Our class yearbook, the 1949 "Mirror," listed every senior's nickname under his or her picture. Under Don Satterfield's name, there is the nickname "Max."

Another new boy, who as I remember arrived when we were in the fifth grade, in Miss Mildred Hettger's class, was the colored boy Aaron Goode. He wasn't in Miss Hettger's class, but in one of two other classes in the fifth grade. Aaron was extremely cheerful and friendly. Where the Goode family came from

I never knew. What I do vividly recall, because it was so remarkable, was that Aaron wore a tie and jacket to school every day. Obviously his parents, sending their boy to a virtually all-white school (only one other classmate, Ann Robinson, was colored), wanted him to represent them and their race well, and so it was tie and jacket every day, the only boy in our grade at Tuscan ever to do as far as I can remember. Aaron wasn't around for long. I know he moved away before even finishing with us at Tuscan, which we did in June, 1943.

Another unusual mode of dress was worn by Jim Stewart, who on certain occasions wore kilts to school. He naturally received some taunting, but as everyone liked him a lot, it was lighthearted kidding only, and certainly did him no damage. Actually, he always wore his kilts proudly.

Just as new arrivals were rare, so were departures. The departures when they did occur did so as follows: The new school year would arrive and on the first day of school we would suddenly notice that so-and-so was no longer there. Could she be sick on the first day of school? After a couple of days, we would realize that she had actually moved away. One such departure, a very sad one for me and many other boys, occurred very early on in our Tuscan days, when one of the two class beauties, blonde Helen Metheny, departed. When Ray Mutter moved just a few miles away, to Chatham, in or after seventh grade, with the exception of one visit back to Maplewood, we never heard of him again. The same was true of the very good athlete Phil Smith, who in or after ninth grade moved to nearby Madison and was never heard from again. It was as if they had moved to Chicago or California instead of to Chatham and Madison.

Walking to school. There were no school busses when I went to the public schools in Maplewood in the 1930s and 1940s. How then, a person of the generations succeeding mine might ask, did we kids get to and from school? The answer, of course, is that we walked.

My route to Tuscan School from my house on Colgate Road was a simple one. All I needed to do was to walk up to the top of Colgate, turn left and walk down Tuscan Road some six or seven streets to the school, and then do the reverse after school to get home. But for a good part of the time that I was at Tuscan that was not the route I took, because Joe Carris and I, inseparable friends and cousins, wanted to walk to school together. Joe and older sister Ada lived at 42 Madison Avenue with parents Milton and Sylvia—my mother's older sister. His house, my house and the school were the points of a large triangle. Although we had not yet studied plane geometry (that came in the tenth grade), Joe and I nonetheless did some geometric work on a street map of Maplewood and located a street corner equidistant between our houses and which was also the shortest distance to Tuscan School. There we would meet each weekday morning and walk to Tuscan together.

In our Tuscan days the school day was divided into morning and afternoon sessions, with everybody going home for lunch. As recounted elsewhere in these pages, Joe and I had lunch together almost every day, alternating between his house and mine. When the school day ended, we would take our respective direct routes home, and I would then walk home with one kid or another, very often with Herbie Roemmele. Going home I usually took not the Tuscan Road route, but Harvard Avenue instead. The latter ran parallel to Tuscan, one street distant from it. At the top of Harvard Avenue was Rutgers Street, and there I would take any one of several shortcuts through backyards to get to Colgate Road.

When I was at Maplewood Junior High School (now known, according to an unwelcome—at least to me—change carried out across the land when we were living abroad, as "Maplewood Middle School") my route was longer. I followed the Tuscan Road route past Tuscan School to the very bottom of the hill where it formed a T-junction with Valley Street. A right/then left dogleg led onto Baker Street, where I continued on to "MJH" with the Maplewood Country Club on my left and Memorial Park on my right.

I must confess that in my seventh grade year at MJH (our initial year there) Herb Roemmele and I quite often got a ride to school along with our friend and neighbor Frank Schoner, who lived on Wellesley Street (his backyard backed onto Herbie's yard). The driver was either Frank's father or mother, and I think that the car was a 1939 Plymouth. Frank's dad was Franklin M. Schoner, Senior. Frank's mom, Maidee (her real name, not a nickname) was a very nice woman who had been Phi Beta Kappa at William and Mary College (I just happen to recall this) and who constantly tried to get Frank to study more and better.

The trek to Columbia High School was considerably longer, but still we usually walked both ways. The route was down Tuscan Road to Prospect Street, thence right on Prospect, many streets along Prospect and lastly left on Parker Avenue to Columbia. Alternatively, I would often take a jagged left turn/right turn route, i.e., taking a jagged hypotenuse and thus eliminating the Tuscan Road and Prospect Street sides of the triangle whose points were my house, the intersection of Tuscan and Prospect, and the intersection of Prospect and Parker.

From time to time I took a bus home from Columbia at the close of the school day. This was *not* a school bus, but a special Public Service Electric and Gas Company (which in addition to providing those two utility services to our part of the state also owned the busses and operated the bus lines) bus which the company provided to serve the school. The fare was a nickel. I never took this bus *to* school, but occasionally took it home after school. The route carried one all the way along Prospect Street to Springfield Avenue, thence down Springfield to the township line on that avenue, just beyond which in neighboring Irvington was the "car barn," the bus's home port (along with all the other Public Service busses).

Finally, I must also admit that in my sophomore or junior year at Columbia, I would often get a ride to school from Dr. William Glickfeld, who was the father of my friend Myron "Midge" Glickfeld, a rough and ready little guy who eventually became a surgeon in Fort Worth, Texas. My fellow passengers were Midge himself, Donny Lester and Frank Rommel, with whom I once had a little run-in which ended well, recounted elsewhere in these pages and who after high school became a U.S. Marine (losing some 50 pounds when he did so) and then a Maplewood policeman. Midge lived at 728 Prospect Street, just near Springfield Avenue, so I would simply walk down Colgate to Springfield, turn right and carry on a few streets along the latter to Prospect and Midge's house, where "Doctor Bill" would drive us to school in his blue 1941 Buick Special two-door.

Forgive the digression; we now return to Tuscan School highlights.

Pearl Harbor Day; my first reactions. On Sunday afternoon, December 7, 1941, I was listening to the New York Giants football game on the radio. Suddenly a voice broke in: "We interrupt this program to bring you a special announcement . . ." It was the "Date of Infamy." My mother was taking a nap when the announcement was made. When she awakened and emerged from her and Dad's bedroom, I excitedly told her: "Mom, we're at war!" Not yet fully awake, she replied, "No kidding?" History reveals that I was not.

The following day, I was at Joe Carris's for lunch between the morning and afternoon sessions at Tuscan School. There we listened to Roosevelt's famous "Date of Infamy" speech on the radio. In the schoolyard, the general assessment of the situation by us fifth and sixth graders (I was in the fifth grade then) was that we would "lick those dirty little Japs in a couple of months." Neither the country nor we kids then realized that it would take not two but forty-five months and the atomic bomb to do so, nor that we would also have to fight a long and terrible war against the Germans as well as against Japan.

We fifth grade patriots were quite willing and ready to do our part, so Herb Roemmele, Joe Carris and I formed the "U.S.J.M.R."—the United States Junior Military Reserve. I must confess that this sterling organization's actual role in the great conflict of World War II was rather modest, in fact non-existent, but the spirit was there! I believe we really thought that we would all be able to join the fray when we got to be a little older. Being kids, and invincible American ones at that, we certainly wanted to. I distinctly remember hoping that the war would last long enough for me to get into it—as a U.S. Marine of course! This desire was further enhanced when I read two of the first books to be written about the war, *Guadalcanal Diary*, by Richard Tregaskis (I have a first edition in my library, with original dust jacket) and *Into the Valley*, by John Hersey.

My first reaction to the war was, I fear, perfectly typical of that of boys and young men throughout history. Their inexperience as to the true nature of war makes them keen to take up arms and experience the adventure of warfare. This has been true at all times in history, whether the time was the start of the Peloponnesian War, 1861, 1914 or 1941.

The "Italian Gang" In 1941, in fifth grade, which means when I was about ten years old, I became aware that there was an "Italian gang" at Tuscan School. The boys in the gang all lived in the Vauxhall section of Maplewood (not at all the good part of our nice suburban township), which comprised some rather depressing streets on both sides of Springfield Avenue, but mainly the notorious "Other Side of Springfield," at Maplewood's very western extremity on the Union border. I think that these boys' parents were all immigrants from Italy or Sicily. Oddly enough, there seemed to be no Italian girls, just the boys (were the girls at parochial schools?).

I looked at (not up to) those lads with a certain amount of awe. They seemed very "tough" to me, very rough and ready guys. I can recall two of them who were in my grade, Sammy Farinella and Bobby Padalino. The other two whom I recall, Joe Farinella (Sam's older brother) and Jimmy Puglio, were a year ahead of me in school. On occasion little Ray Burkhardt, who lived, as mentioned earlier, in what was literally a shack in the Vauxhall section, seemed to hang around (in those days one "hung around;" one did not "hang out") with the Italian gang. Maybe he was their "consigliere straniero."

I noticed that often after school let out the gang members would immediately head for the brook which ran through the school grounds. The brook continued on down the hill, parallel to Tuscan Road, to Valley Street and under it onto the grounds of the Maplewood Country Club. There were fairly steep banks on both sides of the brook, and the land was completely untended by human hands, just growing wild.

I was dying to know what life in this gang could possibly be like, so one day I asked Sammy if I could accompany them one day after school. He told me that he would have to ask his brother Joe. I was quite thrilled when, a few days later, he informed me that I could run with them that very afternoon. All day in class I restlessly looked forward to my after school adventure with this gang, to discovering what went on at the Italians' mysterious conclaves. And what *did* go on? What did we do that afternoon? Why, we walked down the banks above the brook, all the way to Valley Street, simply doing what any and all boys would be doing in such a setting. I was rather disappointed that there was no more to it then that. However, one remarkable event did take place. At one point, Bob Padalino dropped his trousers and did what a bear does in the woods. I had never seen anything like *that* before!

Softball games at Tuscan School. An important feature of daily life at Tuscan School was softball. The school itself kept bats and balls in "the office" (i.e., the office of the principal of the school, the formidable Miss Ireland). We would have choose-up games on the school ball field before school began in the morning and then again after lunch (for which, as mentioned, we always went home, there being no lunch room at Tuscan) before the start of the afternoon session. The players were fifth and sixth graders and the regulars included Herb Roemmele, Joe Carris, myself, Dick Martin, the late Clark MacWright (a big guy a year ahead of me, and a real slugger; I remember him hitting one over the left field fence), Bob Bolster, Ray Mutter, George Wells (also a year ahead and a really fine athlete), *et al.*

One morning, that of either my eleventh or twelfth birthday, i.e., in either fifth of sixth grade, after a night of rain, I arrived at school about thirty minutes early, as usual, ready for softball and feeling great as a birthday boy. In springtime, we softball enthusiasts always came to school early in order to get in a few innings before the start of school. I went to the office to get the bat and ball. However, Miss Ireland had given instructions that, because of wet grounds, we were not to play, so we didn't. Then, after lunch, from which we always rushed back early to get in some more innings before the afternoon session, I went straight to the office to get the bat and ball—Miss Ireland was not there at the time—and we commenced playing. Suddenly, Miss Ireland appeared on the scene. "Did I not tell you this morning that there would be no softball today because the field is wet?" she intoned. "Who came to the office and got the bat and ball?" A score of pairs of eyes turned to me. I could not tell a lie, or should I say I could not have gotten away with telling one. So I 'fessed up, which resulted in Miss Ireland instructing me to come to her office for a little chat. She asked why I had taken the bat and ball from the office and told the others boys it was okay to play when she had very clearly instructed us in the morning that we were not to play because of wet grounds. I muttered my explanation-cum-excuse—that I had not understood that the ban applied to the afternoon, but only to the morning, and that the wet grounds situation should reasonably be reevaluated after lunch. This was rather lame and I knew it was; I was perfectly aware that, had she been there when I went to the office after lunch to fetch the equipment, she would not have permitted it. But seeing as she had *not* been there . . .

In any event, I received a fine lecture on the subject of obedience to legitimate authority, at school and elsewhere, which left me much chastened. I guess the lesson of the lecture sunk in well, inasmuch as I remember the entire incident so very clearly to this day.

The Purple Trio. When I was in the fifth grade at Tuscan School, during the school year 1941-42, my teacher, the truly excellent Miss Mildred Hettger, originated a nickname for me and my two best pals of those years, Joe Carris and Herb Roemmele. The nickname, by which the entire class quickly came to know us, was "The Purple Trio." The reason for the "trio" part of the nickname was a simple one; we were indeed a threesome, constantly "hanging around" with one another. As for the "purple" part, I certainly doubt that she was alluding to our being of royalty or high rank! No, I rather think she had in mind the "vigorous and direct, often offensively so," connotation of the word.

In any event, the nickname certainly endowed its three bearers with a considerable amount of *cachet* in our class from then on. Indeed, as I look back, my fifth year at Tuscan was one of the absolute favorites, not just of my school years, but of my life. 1941 was my first full season as a baseball player and fan. My favorite team, the Brooklyn Dodgers, came out on top after a thrilling pennant race against the Cardinals and won their first pennant in twenty-two years. Also, it was the year the United States entered the Second World War, which we followed closely and found very exciting.

The Damrosch Concerts. It would be rather an exaggeration to state that, in our elementary school days, we Tuscan kids were crazy about classical music. Clearly the appreciation of classical music is something that most children acquire only as they grow into adulthood. I personally did not learn to love such music until I was in my twenties (perhaps I was a bit backward in this respect!). In any event, Tuscan School and its formidable principal, Miss Ruth Ireland, did a good job in at least exposing us to classical music. Periodically, once or maybe twice a month, we went to the school auditorium to listen to the Walter Damrosch Concerts, a popular radio program of the time. A large "console" radio, a Philco, was placed in the center of the stage, facing the audience, i.e., us. It would be tuned to one of the four principal radio stations serving New York, western Connecticut and northern New Jersey in those days—WEAF (660 on the dial), WOR (710), WJZ (770) and WABC (880)—for the Damrosch Concert program of the week. We children of the upper grades, fifth and sixth, would proceed from our classrooms to the auditorium, where we would be seated in alternate seats to ensure we would not be able to talk to one another during the concert. Not really appreciating the music and unable to talk, we were reduced to fidgeting in silence and day dreaming about subjects of interest to us, such as football, baseball, summer vacation and other pleasant and enjoyable things. I should here record a good example of my fifth grade sense of humor; I called the concerts "those damn Rosch concerts."

After school football and baseball. During my fifth and sixth grade years at Tuscan School after-school sports were an important part of our young lives. In the fall it was football and in the spring baseball. The venues for this sports activity were Maplecrest Park, near my house, and Memorial Park, down by Maplewood Junior High, between Valley Street and the Lackawanna railroad tracks.

After school I would go right home to change clothes. One never played in "school clothes." These were, after all, depression years followed by war years, and few families had the wherewithal to waste anything or to be hard on good clothes. Indeed a lot of my clothes were "hand me downs" from my cousin Frank Schreiber (my grandmother's sister Hannah's and "Uncle Lou" Schreiber's son). In the fall, I would don "dungarees," a sweatshirt, shoulder pads, a helmet and "sneakers." That was my football garb. While I was changing, I would listen to 78 r.p.m. records on my wind-up Victrola. My absolute favorite song was "Daddy," the Sammy Kaye version. I played it over and over again. I still love it!

Bill Clingan—a wonderful kid, rough and ready, great fun to be with, a very good friend—would call for me at my house and we would walk over to Maplecrest Park for our afternoon football. Those were the years of that formidable football team, the Martin Maulers, captained by Milward ("Dick") Martin, who was always the tallest boy in our grade, topping out at 6'5" and playing center on the Columbia High School basketball team and also a star swimmer. On the Maulers, *inter alia*, were Joe Carris, Bob Maglie, Quane "Tex" Risinger, Bill Clingan and myself. At this point I should record the words of our "fight" song, composed by Joe Carris and me, to the tune of the Columbia High School football song, "When Our Team is on the Field, Boys."

> "When our team is on the field, boys,
> And the K's (Charley Kimmel's team, our arch rivals) are gettin' a bruise.
> They might was well go home
> Or stay and plan to lose.
> We'll hit them so hard they'll bust,
> In that you all can trust.
> So send up a rousing cheer, boys,
> For the old Martin Maulers!
> Martin, rah! Martin, rah! Maulers, Maulers, rah, rah, rah!"

I hope you will not consider it immodest of me to record the fact that I was a pretty good football player as a boy, with my most successful efforts in the areas of broken field running and intercepting opponents' passes. This despite my very small size; Joe Carris and I were, until high school, always among the smallest boys in our various grades.

We also played football on Saturday mornings down at Memorial Park. I recall that in one such game I broke away for a long run downfield, eluding all tacklers. I was about to cross the goal line, feeling great and proud of my run, not looking behind me, when I was suddenly and unceremoniously tackled from behind and brought down on the two yard line. Who was my intrepid tackler? Why, Herbert Arthur Roemmele, no other!

In the spring after school and of course all summer long, we played baseball at both parks. They were invariably pick-up games and choose-up games, and they certainly were great fun. From age nine onward, I loved baseball more than any sport, both as a player and a fan. I'm still a fan, now, here in 2007. And still a player too, in senior softball leagues.

I think it was in fifth and sixth grades that I played on Charley Kimmel's "Douglas Devils" team (his Uncle Douglas bought our uniforms, the fronts of which were emblazoned with two large capital D's across the chest), at shortstop. Joe Carris played second base. All the other players were a year ahead of us in school, which at that time meant a great deal in terms of ability differentials. I really wasn't ready to play with guys a year older, but I was able to be on the team because as said before, Chuck Kimmel was a pal who lived just up and across the street from me on Colgate Road. Other teammates were Charley, of course, who played catcher, and Bob Szabo, Herman Schactel, Clark MacWright and maybe Dicky Hollander.

Baseball in Maplewood. During the years 1941-44 or thereabouts, Joe Carris and I used to go to Memorial Park after supper, which in those days was at 5:30 or 6:00 pm at the latest, to see baseball games of the Maplewood Twilight League. The players were generally upper year high school boys, college boys and other college-age boys. As I recall, they were in the 17-22 age group. There were five teams in the League—the Concords (who usually won the pennant), the Crescents, the Cardinals, the Bockman A.A. (Athletic Association) and the Maples. I can remember the names of some of the players of those days. The shortstop and captain of the Crescents was our hero, Greg Hillman, son of Aunt Sylvia Carris's friends Ruth and Bayard Hillman (they had another son, Jack, who was also something of a hero to us). On the Cardinals was Jim ("Smokey") Tote, a fastballer (thus the nickname) who I believe later played briefly for the Newark Bears, then the New York Yankees' principal farm team. There were also players named Hank Bogert, Alan Gillick or Killick, the Concords' slugger, who, I remember, did something only rarely done in that league; he hit a homer over the left field fence, which was 305 feet down the left field line, 26 feet more than down the left field line than that of the Polo Grounds. There was first baseman Merrill Box of the Bockman A.A. (Bockman was an automobile dealer, Ford, I think, in Maplewood), who lived on the next street over from Colgate Road, which was Rutgers Street. (Here it should be noted parenthetically that the streets in our section of Maplewood bore the names of colleges and universities, including also Harvard, Yale, Princeton, Wellesley, Oberlin and Bowdoin and, I am sure, some others too). Bill ("Lefty") Scardefield probably pitched for one of the teams, and maybe Bob Roellke (an all-state pitcher for Columbia High School) did too. Although the Concords usually led the league, the Crescents were our favorite because of Greg Hillman.

The American Legion team. Joe Carris and I also attended many Maplewood American Legion team games. Legion ball was for lads up to age sixteen only. I remember that the team wore beautiful white uniforms with stripes, like the Yankees and Bears. I believe the great Roellke pitched for the Legion, as did Johnny Maher and his younger brother Denny. I think Bob Davidson, or was it Jim, was the catcher.

The *Columbia High School* team was also of great interest to me and Joe, long before we ever got to that fine school as students. For the past several years, Joe and I have amused ourselves hugely by thinking of the names of some of the guys who played baseball for Columbia. Here are some of them, in addition to those mentioned above: Tony DeLuca, Pete Cuva, (reputed to have but one testicle), Jack Denardo, Matt Denardo, Charlie Leister, Jack ("Hawk") Burmeister (two of his brothers were in my class at Columbia; both committed suicide at about the same time), Ralph Gamba (a great power hitter), George Garabedian, Ted Fix, "Woozy" Valestin, Eddie Waldron, "Goofy" Deus, and the great Bob Hooper, who made it to the major leagues, the only Maplewood/South Orange player of that era who did so, to my knowledge.

The Tuscan School songs. I think it fitting to end the memories of Tuscan School days with the alma mater and the vacation song. The alma mater lyrics were:

> "Tuscan School is the place for me.
> There's no other school where I'd rather be.
> Loyal and true we'll be to you, dear old Tuscan.
> We will remember so many things,
> The brook in the rain when the waterfall sings.
> And when we're gone, we will think on
> Of dear old Tuscan."

I am indebted to Joe Carris for his invaluable assistance in recalling the words of our school song. The song is brief but quite nice. Now, more than sixty years after leaving dear old Tuscan in June, 1943, I certainly do think on about that lovely school, its many nice kids and the wonderful years, age six through twelve, that I spent there.

As I read the above words to the song, I have the impression that there were more verses. I shall try to think of them and, if there are some and I can later recall them, I'll write them down for the next edition!

The "Vacation" song. Throughout the Tuscan years, during the last week of each school year, we sang a song that we all dearly loved. Here are the words:

"Is there anything you want to know, just ask us we can tell.
We've studied hard for ten long months and we know our lessons well.
But now we're looking for the days when we can have some fun.
For J-u-n-e always spells vaca-a-tion.
So it's hip hip hooray, for the good vacation time.
With an old straw hat, no shoes at all, and a fishing pole and line.
The brook is calling to us and the woods repeat the tune.
The very air, without a care, says June, June June!"

Maplewood Junior High Days. In the fall of 1943, I along with my Tuscan classmates entered Maplewood Junior High. On the first day of seventh grade, I was rather nervous, to say the least. Would I be able to cope with this big school, which incorporated kids from four grade schools—Tuscan, Jefferson, Seth Boyden and half of Fielding (the other half, i.e., the kids who lived east of Parker Avenue, went to South Orange Junior High)? Would I still be as good a student and athlete as I had been at Tuscan, measured against all this new competition? What would it be like to have five different teachers, one for each subject?

Considerable nervousness prevailed during the math class on that first day. Our teacher, Miss Ferguson (affectionately known as "Ma"), started us out with a four-question quiz. We got the results in her class the next day. She read out the names and the scores as she handed the quiz papers back to us. Coming to my name last (I'm certain this was done on purpose) she said, "And Newman, zero. A goose egg! Who is Newman!" The class absolutely roared with laughter, with my pal Herb Roemmele laughing loudest of all. She threw my paper on the floor, from which I in my mortification had to pick it up.

Never mind; in the sixteen "marking periods" of my seventh and eighth grade years, Ma gave me sixteen straight A's in math. And though not wishing to sound immodest I must nonetheless record the fact that in "Denny" Morris's ninth grade algebra class, I tacked on another eight straight A's.

The Eighth and Ninth Grade Athletic Clubs. Early on in my first year, i.e., seventh grade, at Maplewood Junior High School, which is to say in the autumn of 1943, I learned that there were Eighth and Ninth Grade Athletic Clubs, each composed of the twenty-five best athletes (in the estimation of the M.J.H. gym teacher, Mr. John Tice) in those two grades. Athletes then as now were much looked up to by the students in American schools at all levels everywhere in the land, Maplewood of course being no exception. So naturally I very much hoped to be selected for these athletic clubs, known then and now as "A.C.s." But was I good enough? I had been among the better athletes in Tuscan School, but now the competition would be much tougher; there were boys from three other schools, Jefferson, Seth Boyden and Fielding, in my seventh grade class and of course in eighth and ninth as well. One day in my seventh grade year, George Morgan, the older brother of Gilbert Morgan, one of the neighborhood boys of roughly my age (the Morgan family lived on Rutgers Street next and parallel to Colgate Road), told me that "you have to be very good to make the Eighth Grade A.C." This was at a time when I secretly dreamed of making that very club. I think George's words were his way of informing me that he didn't think I was good enough to make it, and they certainly deflated my hopes.

So much so that when I entered eighth grade in the fall of 1944 I thought I had no chance of making the eighth grade club. During seventh grade sports activities, I had seen how much better than I a good number of the guys from the other elementary schools were and so I did not even submit an application for admission to the club.

During the days of autumn at M.J.H., "gym" (i.e., physical education) class for boys consisted of touch football games in nearby Memorial Park, to which we would walk for a game of some forty-five minutes duration. One fine September day in such a game of "touch" I intercepted three passes in about ten minutes, making good runbacks each time. After my third interception, Mr. Tice, who watched our games sitting on a bench atop a little hillock at the side of the playing field, blew his whistle, stopping the action on the field. "Joe Newman," he called, "come up here." I did so. He then totally astonished and delighted me by asking, "Joe, why haven't you put in your application for the Eighth Grade Athletic Club?" I stammered something like, "Well, I didn't know if I was good enough, sir." "Put in your application," he commanded. I of course did so and was soon thereafter selected to be a member of the exalted group.

Our coach was not Mr. Tice—he coached the Ninth Grade A.C.—but Mr. Dennis Morris, a mathematics teacher at the school. Mr. Morris not incorrectly judged that I was a better math student than a first-string athlete. He put me on the fourth team in basketball, the A.C.'s major sport. I was very small for my age (thirteen entering eighth grade, turning fourteen on March 26 of that 1944-45 school year), obviously a significant disadvantage to a basketball player. Perhaps at a stretch I might have been good enough to be on the third team, a big difference from the fourth in terms of prestige, but Denny (as we all called him, *not* to his face) didn't think so.

As I recall, and I think I do so accurately, the top ten players on the A.C. (i.e., the first and second teams) were Don Ronnie, Dick Martin, Bob Schneider, Eddie Horbelt, Johnny Horbelt, "Tex" Risinger, Griff Amerman, Donny Campbell, Murdock Merchant and George Cain. One name conspicuously absent from the 9th grade club was that of Dick Witzig, whom Mr. Tice rather inexplicably and stubbornly failed to name to the club. I believe the coach's rationale in the case of Dick was that he was "too small." That made no sense because Bob Olwine, Bill Zwigard and I were also very little guys, no taller than Dick. Since Dick

Witzig is a first-class guy and a friend with whom I am in contact to this very day, indeed an esteemed and valued friend, I shall allow myself to relate this vignette about him.

Mr. Tice had posted on the bulletin board in the boys' locker room the list of those who had made the Ninth Grade A.C. Standing next to me as we looked at it was Dick, age fourteen, like myself. When he looked in vain for his last name and found it not there, he walked slowly away, fighting back tears. I felt very bad for him; he surely deserved to be on the club.

Dick's reaction was to work very hard at practicing his favorite sport over the ensuing months and as a result he got better and better. So much so that when we entered Columbia High School the next school year, in the fall of 1946, he made the "jayvee" (i.e., j.v., for junior varsity) basketball team. He thereafter made the varsity team and in our senior year the first team varsity! Almost a half a century later, when we got together on one of my frequent trips to California, Dick related to me a wonderful denouement to the story of his rejection by Mr. Tice. Before each Columbia basketball game, the varsity would be led out onto the court by a member of the team. On a certain occasion Dick led the team out, of course dribbling nicely as he did so. In the stands for the game was John Tice. Dick stopped, continuing to dribble, turned and looked directly into the eyes of Mr. Tice for a delicious moment or two, then dribbled on. Revenge is a dish best tasted cold!

Back to the Eighth Grade A.C. Whom did we play against? Our opponents were the teams of the various ninth grade homerooms. A special event was the annual game against the Ninth Grade A.C. played at night with parents present. I played for a few minutes and did not disgrace myself.

I have some trouble remembering whom the Ninth Grade A.C. played their games against. I'll hazard a guess that our opponents were teams from the various Columbia High School tenth grade homerooms. Somehow that doesn't sound right to me, however. But who else could we have played against?

Chattanooga Choo-Choo. I don't know whether it was done only once or several times but some time in the winter of 1945-46 Mr. John Morgan, a teacher of American history at Maplewood Junior High, organized and directed a minstrel show with a cast composed primarily of ninth graders. In these days of ever-so-annoying "political correctness" (which in this observer's view is in actuality a morose kind of intellectual obtuseness) minstrel shows are *verboten*, *interdit*. But it was fine and fun back then and those of us who were in the show gave it our all, with pretty good results.

Mr. Morgan held tryouts for the show. Nobody was rejected. Those with the best acts were featured, while those who had no act to put on but wanted to participate formed the chorus. Mr. Morgan sat in the middle of the front row as the interlocutor and the entire cast of course wore blackface.

Joe Carris and I devised a pretty good rendition of "Chattanooga Choo-Choo," the great and to this day, very delightful and popular Glen Miller hit of the war years. For our act I dressed in a way that was then called "sharp," with—I remember it very well—a maroon shirt borrowed from my dad, light-colored trousers and one of his hats. Cousin Joe was the shoeshine boy, dressed in some raggedy clothes and carrying the shoeshine kit which as noted before I had received as a birthday present in my pre-school days and which remained in use by me even into my early adulthood.

The only musical accompaniment was provided by the highly talented Doug Williams on piano. Joe and I sang out the lyrics as follows:

Joe N.:	"Pardon me, boy, is that the Chattanooga Choo-Choo?"
Joe C.:	"Yass, yass, track twenty-nine!"
Joe N.:	"Boy, you can give me a shine."
Joe C.:	"Can you afford to board the Chattanooga Choo-Choo?" (Rather uppity kind of question, no?)
Joe N.:	"I've got my fare, and just a trifle to spare."
Joe C.:	"You leave the Pennsylvania station 'bout a quarter to four (a shoeshine boy providing train information!), read a magazine and then you're in Baltimore." (Did it not occur to this waif that his customer might prefer The New York Times or Herald Tribune to a magazine?)
Both of us:	"Dinner in the diner, nothing could be finer, than to have your ham and eggs in Carolina."
Joe C.:	"When you hear the whistle blowin' eight to the bar, then you'll know that Tennessee is not very far."
Both of us:	"Shovel all the coal in, gotta keep it rollin' Woo-Woo Chattanooga there you are!"
Joe N.:	"There's gonna be a certain party at the station. (Telling this to a shoeshine boy!)
Joe C.:	"Satin and lace?" (Another ill-mannered question.)
Joe N.:	I used to call 'Funny Face'. She's gonna cry until I tell her that I'll never roam." (Telling this to a shoeshine boy was not only indiscreet but absolutely out of order).
Both of us:	"So Chattanooga Choo-Choo, won't you choo-choo me home!"

Would you believe thunderous applause?

"Two Irishmen." In the late spring or, more likely, the summer of '44, after seventh grade at Maplewood Junior High School, Joe Carris and I one day rode our bicycles up to Sagamore Road to see Dick Witzig and Donny Campbell, who lived next door to each other on that street. They taught us a song which we sang all the way home, and often thereafter. It went as follows:

"Two Irishmen, two Irishmen, were digging in a ditch.
One called the other a dirty son-of-a-b_ _ _ _.
Peter Murphy, Peter Murphy sitting on a rock.
Along came a bumblebee and stung him on the
Cocktails, ginger ale, five cents a glass,
And if you don't like it
You can shove it up your
Ask me no questions, I'll tell you no lies.
If you ever get hit with a bucket of s_ _ _
Don't forget to close your eyes."

Charming, no?

The Whippets. When I was about fourteen or fifteen years old, to be a member of an exclusive little group of guys, or "club," was very much the thing to do. One day Joe Carris and I decided that we should form such a club. For us there was the model of some older guys we looked up to, who had a club named the Ponums. The Ponums were my Colgate Road neighbor Caesar Kimmel, Joe's Madison Avenue neighbor Dick Cherry, plus Kenny Winters and Jack Steigerwald.

Needing some other members for our club (*only* a few, for reasons of exclusivity), we selected some guys we were buddies with at the time—Peter Eisenman, Mike Spicer, Don Brief, Bob Brody and Bob Ellis. These worthies were of course glad to join us. The first order of business was to select and bestow upon ourselves an appropriate name. The selection process was simple. We got hold of a book about the various breeds of dogs; it listed them all and had photographs of each. We poured over the pages seeking just the right one for our purposes. How about "The Bulldogs?" No good; that was Yale or Georgia. "The German Shepherds?" Certainly not; the year was 1944 or 1945 and the Germans were the hated enemy. How about "The Collies?" No, that wouldn't do either. Then, towards the end of the book, we came across the perfect name, that of a breed which neither Joe nor I had ever heard of—the Whippet. Apparently this breed was small and fast, which is just what Joe and I actually were—small—and what we wanted to be—fast! And so the Whippets were born. This grouping lasted for almost a full year, until we got to Columbia High School, where as high school "men" we allowed our little club to die through neglect.

My Introduction to New Orleans jazz. One evening during the summer of 1946, between my graduation from Maplewood Junior High School and my starting at Columbia High School, I somehow happened to be in a store in the shopping area of Springfield Avenue by Prospect Street, a store which among other things sold record albums. In those days, a record album consisted of four 78 r.p.m. records in a hard cardboard book-like folder with four record sleeves inside. At the record counter of the store, my attention was attracted to an interesting cover on an album of Jelly Roll Morton (as of that moment I had no idea who he was). The cover showed a Negro playing an upright piano on the street floor of a house in the French Quarter of New Orleans. I bought the album, took it home, and played each of the records on my little wind-up "Victrola." I was thunderstruck by the music, which of course was New Orleans jazz, known also as Dixieland jazz. I absolutely loved it at first hearing. What is more, I still love it as I write these words sixty years later.

I no longer have those records, unfortunately, but I do have a tape of Jelly Roll and his wonderful band, a tape with sixteen mastered versions of most of the numbers on my album's records plus some others. It's a terrific tape, one which I listen to frequently. Included on it are Sidewalk Blues, Dead Man Blues and Kansas City Stomp. Listening to this wonderful music by the great Jelly Roll and his fine jazz men always invokes in my mind memories of those precious days when I first began listening to and loving Dixieland. It was a true revelation for me.

Entering Columbia High School. It was not without some trepidation that, on a beautiful sunny day in early September of 1946, I got up, dressed neatly and carefully, had breakfast with sister Rho in the "breakfast nook" of our kitchen, and walked (with Herb Roemmele, as I recall) to Columbia High—one of the finest public high schools in America—for my first day of school there. It was a glorious early September day and an important one; I was now a high school "man."

At the outset of the school day we reported to our respective "homerooms," mine being that of Mr. Wenker. As the day progressed, we went to our various classes, each of which lasted just under an hour, with a few minutes in between, during which brief intervals we made our way through the corridors from one class to another. For the record, my courses were plane geometry, taught by Mr. Melotte; Spanish, Mrs. Ahern; Latin, Miss Caswell (who also served as our class guide) English; and physical education, popularly known as "gym" and of course a great favorite with us boys.

Columbia was a relatively large school because it was attended not only by Maplewood boys and girls but also those from neighboring South Orange. My class comprised almost five hundred students, the school almost fifteen hundred.

This was a bit daunting for the first few days, but we quickly adjusted to the larger school environment; our school spirit and sense of belonging were quickly enhanced as football season began and we went to Underhill Field on Saturdays to cheer for the Cougars.

A Couple of Disappointments. At the end of classes on that first exciting day at Columbia I quickly got myself over to Underhill Field to try out for "jayvee" (junior varsity) football. I was then fifteen and a half years old, about five feet and a couple of inches tall, and weighed in at about one hundred thirty-five pounds soaking wet—not exactly a big guy who would terrify opponents on the gridiron! (I should record that I caught up in size with most of my male counterparts during my years at Columbia; I was about five feet eleven inches tall and weighed about one hundred sixty-five pounds when I graduated).

In any event I managed to hang in there during the daily practice sessions, surviving the first "cut." But *not* the last cut, in which I was dropped from the squad with a number of other hopefuls. This was of course a big disappointment to someone—me—who was absolutely crazy about sports. As previously noted, at Maplewood Junior High I had been a member of both the Eighth and Ninth Grade Athletic Clubs. At Columbia, however, the competition was twice as tough because now we also had the best athletes from South Orange Junior High in our class, and needless to say there were more than a few really good ones among them.

Not long after not making the jayvee football team, I tried out for jayvee basketball. On the first day of practice, looking around me at the large number of classmates who were also trying out, I tried to make a realistic assessment of my chances of making the team. In the Ninth Grade Athletic Club I had been on the fourth team—hardly an exalted position. Now at Columbia I had to compete not only against the best from Maplewood but also against the best from South Orange. As I recall, about forty tenth grade boys tried out for the jayvees, which squad after the final cut would be reduced to twelve, or fifteen at most. So looking at my chances in a realistic way didn't fill me with confidence that I would make the team. But hope springs eternal, so I turned up for practice in the Columbia gym day after day and played as well as I could. In fact I didn't play badly at all and so I lasted until the final cut when reality caught up with me and I was cut. This was a big disappointment! Which of my Ninth Grade A.C. teammates *did* make the Columbia jayvees? As I recall, the boys who made the team were (not in any kind of rank order) George Cain, Murdock Merchant, the Horbelt twins, Dick Martin, Don Ronnie, Don Campbell and Dick Witzig (who, as I have recounted, inexplicably had not been named to the Ninth Grade A.C. by its coach, John Tice, but who nonetheless became a stellar member of the Columbia varsity basketball team in our junior and senior years).

One learns to live with disappointments. They are part of life. What counts most is the grace with which one accepts and surmounts them.

Dating. This was an important teenage folkway and rite of passage in our junior high school and high school days, I think more so than now, when teenagers generally seem to "hang out" in packs rather than go out on boy-girl dates.

I myself was shy vis-à-vis girls during those years—very much so at the outset in junior high, gradually less so as the years passed, not at all when I went off to college. In those early years I had to work up courage just to call a girl on the phone and ask her for a date. In fact I didn't manage to accomplish this until I was fourteen years old, in eighth grade. I called one M.M., a girl as nice as she was pretty, on the phone and invited her to go to the movies with me. She accepted and on a Friday night we went to one of the "first run" movie houses in downtown Newark (there were four of these: the Paramount, RKO Proctors, Loews and the Branford). It took me a good hour to screw up my courage to hold her hand and—*mirabile dictu*—when I did so she didn't reject this bold advance! After the movie, we went to a "soda fountain" for "black and white" sodas. I certainly would have liked to kiss her good night at her front door, but that would have required more courage than I was able to muster.

Social life became more active during my ninth grade year. That was when girls began giving parties at their homes, with mothers and others of course present in chaperone capacity. These parties followed a set routine. At the outset the girls would be together talking among themselves, while the boys would do the same. I'm not sure what the girls talked about, but we boys talked about—sports! All of us would be drinking Coca-Cola and nibbling pretzels, peanuts and potato chips. Then, after some thirty or forty minutes some bold guy would ask some sweet damsel to dance and soon after we would all be dancing. As the evening wore on the lights would be turned down low and "cheek-to-cheek" dancing would begin. Some couples actually kissed during this dancing, but not this writer, still too shy for that sort of thing.

I remember quite distinctly the first time I kissed a girl. This happened down at the Jersey shore during the summer of 1947, after my sophomore year (i.e., first) year at Columbia. The girl in question was one J.H. (as in the case of M.M. above, initials must be used to protect the innocent), a pretty brunette. Now that was truly a thrill!

Dancing Classes. It was during the ninth grade (the final year of junior high) that Joe Carris and I were enrolled in dancing classes at the Emily Sarles School of the Dance, located on the second floor, above stores, of a building on the west side of the avenue in South Orange Village. We learned the fox trot, the waltz, the lindy hop, and maybe the rhumba. Now here's a fact that today seems quite strange, not to say almost unbelievable. There were two separate classes at Emily Sarles', one for Christian kids, the other for Jewish kids. That kind of thing was simply a fact of life in 1940s America. There was an almost complete separation of Christian and Jewish kids when it came to dating and parties. Relationships between the two groups were entirely friendly and cordial in all areas of school life, but not in the out-of-school social arena. That's not to say that relationships were unfriendly in the social life sphere; they were just non-existent. I search my memory trying to recall *any* time a Jewish guy went out with a Christian girl, or vice versa. I'm sure it must have happened on occasion, but only rarely. When I told my own kids about this, they found it almost impossible to believe. But my classmates who read this will recall that that's the way it was back then.

My first date in a car. A car driven by *me*, that is. Shortly after getting my driver's license a few days after my seventeenth birthday, which is to say in the early spring of 1948, I managed to persuade my father to let me use my mother's car, a nice 1947 Oldsmobile two-door "coupe," to go out on a date. Of course this was a major milestone in my then young life. The girl in question was a pretty and charming brunette by the name of Joan, who lived not in Maplewood but just over the township line in Irvington. After dressing smartly (the wearing of a tie and jacket on such an occasion was *de rigeur*, indeed almost mandatory, in those days—a custom which I daresay American youth would have been well advised to continue but of course did not!) I jumped into the car and, feeling very much the young man about town, headed out to call for my date.

I was driving down Springfield Avenue, approaching the traffic light at the intersection of Boyden Avenue, when I made the major error of taking my eyes off the road in front of me for just a second or two. When I looked back to where I never should have stopped looking, I was amazed and shocked to see an oil delivery truck looming up in front of me. I braked hard and fast but too late. I crashed into the back of the truck, doing no damage to the truck but smashing in the grille of my mom's car. After the exchange of licenses and insurance details with the driver of the truck, I continued on my way to pick up the lovely Joan, feeling quite deflated as well as quite apprehensive about what my father's reaction would be when he saw the smashed-in grille of Mom's Olds.

What a great guy my dad was, and what a perfect kind of father (I can say exactly the same thing about my mom—a great gal and a perfect mother). The next morning, when I told him about the accident and the damage to the car, all he said was something about the importance of always remaining fully alert while driving and even more so at night, suggesting (actually, of course, it was a mandate) that I not drive Mom's car at night for a couple of months, until I had acquired more experience as a driver.

Gruning's. There cannot have been many Columbia High School students in the 1940s who did not at least occasionally go to Mr. Herman Gruning's renowned ice cream parlor during their high school years. Many, like myself and any number of my friends and acquaintances went often, not necessarily to consume a Coke, ice cream soda or sundae but just because it was the place to go after school unless you were a "jock," who had to go to practice after school, or one who had to stay on at the school after classes for some other extra-curricular activity, such as I did during my senior year when I was editor-in-chief of the Mirror, our class yearbook. A look at that publication's 1949 edition will reveal how I appeared in my pre-Ivy League look days, with pompadour hair style and a rather dreadful necktie tied in a Windsor knot. For the record, I should record the prices of the above-mentioned Gruning specialties: small Coke, a nickel; ice cream soda, fifteen cents; ice cream sundae, twenty-five cents; and a very special sundae called a "banana royal," thirty-five cents.

One of the reasons why Gruning's was the place to go was that it was the venue where we boys could look at the girls and even talk to them and maybe even buy them a soda. And although I obviously can't speak for the girls, I suspect that they went there at least in part to look at and be seen by the boys, talk to them, and be treated to a soda.

Being an entrepreneurial businessman, Mr. Gruning in the late 1940s opened another establishment, this one more of a restaurant and family-type place called "The Top," located on South Orange Avenue a few streets above Wyoming Avenue and South Mountain School. But this was not the same as his village emporium and so never really attained any significant status as a "hangout." Instead it was the kind of place you went to with your parents and siblings for dinner from time to time (*not* frequently in those pre-eat out regularly days).

I particularly recall two events that occurred at or in front of Gruning's. One was a fist fight *inside* the place during my senior year, the participants being myself and a boy by the name of . . . well, there's no need to identify him. The outcome of these fisticuffs? Just let me say that it would be something of an exaggeration, not to say incorrect, if I were to claim that I won this fight, for the lad in question landed two punches on me to my none landed on him before other boys stepped in and broke up the bout. What was the reason for this fight? We were both vying for the affections of a pretty and perky blonde belle, which led to certain hot words being spoken that would more sensibly not have been spoken!

The other event was an external one that took place some miles away in Brooklyn, the progress of which, as reported by the great "Red" Barber, a bunch of us were following by means of a portable radio on the sidewalk in front of Gruning's. This was the famous Dodgers-Yankees 1947 World Series game in which Floyd ("Bill") Bevens no-hit the Dodgers for eight and two-thirds innings, only to lose both his no-hitter and the game when Harry ("Cookie") Lavagetto lashed a pinch hit double off the wall in the last half of the ninth inning to drive in two runs and give the Brooks an historic 2 to 1 victory. That was a moment of great joy for me, devout Dodger fan that I was, and for millions of other devoted followers of "the Flock." On the other hand it was the cause of great chagrin for those who were Yankee fans, but needless to say the Bronx Bombers won the Series anyway, as indeed they won every Series against the Dodgers until that hallowed year of 1955, when the magnificent pitching performances of Johnny Podres and the heroics of little Sandy Amoros, whose unbelievable catch, after an incredible dash of some fifty yards to catch up with the ball, of Yogi Berra's seemingly sure double resulted in a rally-crushing, game-winning double play. I know I'm digressing but I want to record that that seventh game of the 1955 Series was one of the high points of my life up to that time, perhaps surpassed only by my entry into the world on March 26, 1931; my being elected to membership in the exalted Friars Senior Society at Penn; my meeting and marrying my wonderful Greta, who was good enough to marry me on June 5, 1954 and then to make my life a supremely happy one during forty-four years of marriage until her untimely death in June 1998; and my meeting and marrying my present wonderful wife, Sue Della Corte, with whom I'm looking forward to spending another twenty happy years!

An abortive overnight. One weekend night during my Columbia High School days, I and four or five other guys, after an evening of doing something or other like going to a movie or playing poker, were invited by our classmate Johnny Sugarman to stay overnight at his house in South Orange. So six blankets and six pillows were spread out on the living room floor of the Sugarman residence and undressing down to our skivvie shorts and T-shirts we flopped down for a night's sleep. But first of course we had to talk, joke and kid around for a while. The noise we were making soon attracted the attention of Mr. Sugarman, who from the outset had not been very pleased at the idea of his son and five of his buddies sleeping on his living room floor but had been persuaded by Mrs. Sugarman, quite against his will, to permit the overnight. Mr. Sugarman was if anything not a very easygoing, catch-as-catch-can, let 'er rip kind of man. On the contrary, one could even describe him as rather austere. The poor man merely wanted to go to sleep peacefully in his bedroom of a Saturday night. The idea of six boys making nuisances of themselves on his living room floor into the wee hours had probably not been part of his plans for that night. So from the top of the stairs he told us in no uncertain terms that if we did not immediately shut up and go to sleep he would without further ado evict us all (except, of course, Johnny himself), the late hour notwithstanding.

Did we shut up and go to sleep? Of course not. We continued to talk and joke and laugh and make noise for several minutes. Not surprisingly, Mr. Sugarman appeared at the top of the stairs once again. His manner was peremptory: "Out—all of you—now!" he announced. "I'll deal with you in the morning, Johnny." And so out into the street we went, feeling a bit sorry for Johnny, who was last seen pleading with his father, saying imploringly: "But, Dad, you can't just put my friends out into the street at 2:00 a.m." Oh, yes he could. And did!

It was a long walk home.

Poker games. Poker games were very popular among a group of my Columbia High School classmates during our years there, autumn 1946-June 1949. To name a few, the regulars included Jimmy Steiner, Rich Pollack, Billy Leeds, Bob Turk, Joe Carris, Stan Greene, and myself. The games (we called them "tilts") were arranged in two ways. The formal method was that one of the guys would say: "Let's have a game at my house on Friday night," and would get a bunch together for that purpose. On a rainy, snowy or otherwise cold day on which back yard basketball (actually it was driveway basketball, with the backboard and basket attached to the front of the garage) was not appropriate, a tilt might be arranged in the school halls between classes, or at lunch in the cafeteria or at Gruning's after school. We would then proceed to the house of the guy who had volunteered to host the game that day.

We played several variations of the game of poker. The most popular were five-card draw and seven-card stud. The stakes were always the same, "nickel/dime." Thus on a good night the "big winner" might be ahead something on the order of seven or eight dollars and the "big loser" out a similar amount. Remember that those were the days when an eight-slice pizza at a stand known as "the shack" cost one dollar, hot dogs a dime, Cokes and Pepsis a nickel, cigarettes twenty cents a pack, and tuition at Harvard, Yale, Penn, *et al.*, four hundred dollars a year!

Three particular incidents come to mind when I recall those poker games. The first occurred on a very rainy afternoon at my house at 21 Colgate Road. On that particular day, an unusually large number of fellows wanted to play, and there were no less than three separate games in progress on the first floor of our seven-room "Dutch Colonial"—one at the dining room table, a second at the table in the alcove off the kitchen called the "breakfast nook," and a third on the living room floor. As the games were going on, my father returned from work and entered the front door, then tried to open the inner, vestibule door, which led to the living room. Alas, he encountered a slight difficulty in opening this door because there was a body on the other side of it. Not a corpse, mind you, just a prone poker player. Was Dad amused? Actually not; perhaps he had had a bad day at the office. Finally managing to gain admission to his house, Dad took one look around him and said calmly but softly, "Out, everybody out." And out they went, and quickly too. The reader should bear in mind that my father was an easygoing and friendly man who liked my friends and was widely liked and admired by them. Well, some aggravation at the office accompanied by a wretched rainy day can sour just about anybody's mood, even Al Newman's!

The second incident I recall took place, I believe, on a weekend evening at the home of Stuart Albert (not a classmate, but one or two years ahead of us "Forty-niners" at Columbia) in the Montrose section of South Orange. I know almost for certain who was playing that night. The protagonists (antagonists during the incident) were Billy Leeds, Rich Pollack and Jim Steiner. Also present were Stu, Joe Carris, maybe Barry Lippman, and myself. The incident took place on what turned out to be the last hand of the night, a two-card high/low game. Four of us had dropped out, Jimmy had declared low (and so couldn't lose), while both Billy and Rich had declared high and were really duking it out. Rich would bet a dime, Bill would call, and Jimmy of course would raise a dime. Then Rich would raise it another dime, Billy would again call, and Jimmy of course would raise it again. This went on for several rounds, after which Billy said: "This is getting ridiculous. Call, Jimmy." Rich retorted: "Don't you dare call, Jimmy. I've got ten more dollars in my pocket and I'm going to bet it all." Billy continued saying, "Call, Jimmy, call," and finally Jim did so. Rich, who had been bluffing with an ace and a picture card, or twenty-one, was the loser to Billy's two-picture pair, and was furious. "I'll never play cards with you again, Jimmy Steiner," said he, stalking out of the house. He went to start up the car in which he had driven to Stu's house, his mother's Dodge (or perhaps it was a Chrysler) convertible. With that—boom! Off went the harmless little fireworks bomb someone (I can't remember who, but it wasn't me) had put in the car's engine, set to go off when the car was started up. Richard came back into the house and with an icy stare and in an icier voice said, "Which of you jokers put a bomb in my mother's car?" The rest of us tried unsuccessfully to suppress smiles. Rich was fuming angry, but of course he got over it in a day or two. I think we played again the next weekend and, needless to say, both Rich and Jim were in the game, friendly as ever.

The third incident was a truly nasty one. It also took place at my house one fine day, during an after-school game. A new boy (who shall remain nameless in this recounting) had recently moved to South Orange from Newark and had become a regular participant in our poker games. He astonished us all by winning constantly, almost never losing, and getting outstanding hands in five-card draw—three-of-a-kind and full houses—an inordinate number of times. What a lucky guy, we all thought. On the day in question, this new guy was about to deal a hand of five-card draw when Stan Greene, a really good poker player as well as a man with a watchful eye, grabbed the deck out of his hand. "Watch this," said Stan. "I'm going to deal 'em out and you'll see three-of-a-kind in front of _ _ _ _ _ _." In a dramatic fashion, Stan dealt five cards to each of us and, lo and behold, there were three queens in front of _ _ _ _ _ _. He had stacked the deck when "washing" it prior to his deal (Note: We always used two decks, and the next to deal would mix the just-used deck for the next hand), and had been doing so right from the very first time he joined our games.

There was a time and place in our country's past when what _ _ _ _ _ _ did might easily have resulted in his being shot and killed, but luckily for him such was no longer the case. Needless to say, however, no one was very keen to play with that particular character again and he was of course excluded from our games in the future. I recall this incident ever so clearly more than half a century later, which only goes to show that "the evil that men do lives after them."

Columbia High School football cheers and songs. To this day I remember some Columbia cheers and songs. I am proud to say I have taught them to all my grandchildren, who can recite them with fervor, much to their parents' chagrin.

The following is not a complete list, but just the ones I remember. (Note: the first was sung to the tune of Columbia University's "Roar, Lion, Roar.")

Roar, Cougar, Roar
Roar, Cougar, roar
And wake the echoes of the Orange Valley.
Fight on to victory evermore,
Every loyal son and daughter
Rally 'round, Columbia, Columbia,
Shouting her name forever.
Roar, Cougar, roar,
Our alma mater praised be evermore.

Cheer, Columbia Spirit
Cheer, Columbia spirit!
None can prevail.
Follow our colors,
They will never fail.
Rah, rah, rah,
We are not divided.
None us defy.
Our alma mater,
Columbia High!

Alla-Veevo
Alla-veevo, all-vyvo, alla-veevo-vyvo-vess.
Come seven, come eleven,
Come a rickety-rackety shanty town
Who can pull Columbia down?
Nobody, nobody, yea!
Nobody, nobody, yea!
When you're up you're up
When you're down you're down
When you're up against Columbia
You're upside down
Hit 'em in the head
Hit 'em in the feet
Columbia High School can't be beat!

Chicka-Lacka
Chicka-lacka, chicka-lacka, chow chow chow!
Booma-lacka, booma-lacka, bow wow wow!
Chicka-lacka, booma-lacka, sis boom bah!
Columbia High School, rah rah rah!

These songs and cheers were of course led by our school cheerleaders (males), resplendent in white trousers, white shirts, red sweaters and white shoes, and utilizing red megaphones.

And here's one that I remember part but I think not all of:

Good Night Poor _ _ _ _ _ _ _ _ _
Good night, poor Kearny (or Plainfield, Morristown, etc.)
Kearny, good night.
We've got your number
You're high as a kite.
When the Big Red team gets after you
Kearny, good night.

I think there were some other lines after "kite" and before "when the Big Red team."

Applying to colleges and universities. My Columbia High School classmates and I became seniors in 1948. This was the time when the serious process of applying to college got underway. The first thing a senior had to do, of course, was to decide which college (I use the generic term "college" to include both colleges and universities) he or she wanted to attend. Then one had to get through the various elements of the application for admission process. First, one filled out a lengthy application form and sent it to the admissions offices in question along with a photo (now forbidden under the stringent strictures of political correctness) and the application fee, usually twenty-five to fifty dollars. The application forms asked for one's sex, race, religion (also prohibited now). Second, one took the Scholastic Aptitude Test and one or more Scholastic Achievement Tests. Third, one had the "office" at Columbia send in a transcript of one's grades, then called "marks," in the various high school courses one had taken. Finally most colleges required letters of recommendations which as a general rule came from one's father's best friend, employer or employee, from one's uncle (never identified as such, of course), or from one's minister, priest or rabbi. Once the application process had been completed, all we could do was carry on with our lives and nervously hope for the best.

I applied to the University of Pennsylvania, Lehigh, and William and Mary. Penn was my first choice, the other two just in case Penn wouldn't take me (which negative outcome I considered unlikely but certainly possible). In the event I was accepted by all three. I of course chose Penn. When I matriculated (the word we used then; I wonder if it is still used) at Penn, I was accompanied by a good number of my classmates from Columbia's class of 1949: Bob Turk (my close pal then and for more than a half a century, and counting, since then); Barry Lippman, Arnie Pomerantz, Sumner Williams, Bernie Salinger (no relation to Pierre as far as I know), Paul Ehrlich (of "Zero Population Growth" and "The Population Time Bomb" fame or notoriety, and arch-enemy of the noted conservative economist the late Julian Simon, himself a 1949 graduate of the high school in the next-door town of Millburn), *et al.*

Yale also took a large contingent of Columbia Forty-niners: my close pal and first cousin Joe Carris (who throughout his school years was known by his first name, Sol. Joseph was his middle name; he escaped the former appellation only when he went on to Yale), Lyle Brundage; Bill Dudley; Ralph Miller; Ludwig Pietz; Alan Pois; Walter Beaney, and Bob Agman. This was an exceptionally large intake of boys for Yale to take from a single public high school, because Yale in those days (and no doubt still) tended to favor prep school boys, who were in many cases the sons of Yale alumni. Harvard also took several of my classmates, not surprisingly in every case boys who were "brains," i.e., straight-A students, at Columbia: Stan Greene (who, if he hadn't needed to study long and hard so as to get a necessary scholarship and thus couldn't go out for basketball, would have been a varsity player for Columbia in that sport); Harold Silverman and a couple of others.

Rounding out the Big Three, Barrett ("Spike") Hazeltine went to Princeton. And rounding out the Ivy League contingent, Jimmy Steiner went to Columbia,

Rich Pollack to Brown and Bob Morris to Dartmouth. I can't recall if any of us went to Cornell. Off to Williams went another good-sized group: Peter Sterling; Donny Campbell; George Cain and Milward ("Dick") Martin. To Colgate went Griff Amerman, Ted von Glahn and Johnny Horbelt. And to Hamilton College went Bob Olwine.

Lehigh also took a good contingent: Herb Roemmele; Dick Witzig; Jim Lebo; Art Tauck; Jerry Hannay. Amos Plante and Bill Clingan went to Purdue. Finally, Denny Lafer went to Haverford and "Midge" Glickfeld to Tulane. This is of course only a partial list. A large majority of our class, both boys and girls, went on to higher education. I believe our class was an exceptional one in this and other respects.

The reader will notice two things about the above list. First, I can't think of a single guy, other than Midge, who went to college in the Far West, Southwest or South. I know that some of my classmates must have gone to colleges in at least one of those areas, but I'm unable to think of any others who did. That strikes me as quite remarkable. Second, there is no mention of girls in the list. The reason for this is *not* that Columbia girls didn't go on to college, because the majority did. It's just that where they went simply didn't register in the mind or consciousness of the writer. A reasonable and charitable explanation for this is that such was simply the way things were in those days. Almost all the schools mentioned above took boys only. In addition, where girls went to college didn't seem important then because what they were going to be after college were not business executives, doctors, dentists, lawyers or engineers, but wives and mothers. I must now direct the following comment to all distaff members of the class of 1949; the way it is now is the way it *ought* to be, and I am in fact sympathetic to equity (as opposed to gender) feminism.

Summer jobs. In my high school and college days it was an important thing to get a summer job between school years. It was simply not considered the right thing to do to just "hang around" during summer vacation. Summer jobs were very much the thing to do, very *de rigeur*, and I had one every summer from that of 1947 (the year of Jackie Robinson's historic and momentous rookie year with the Brooklyn Dodgers) through that of 1953, after my graduation from Penn and before my abortive first year at Harvard Law School.

My first summer job, covering late June-late August 1947, was after my sophomore (first) year at Columbia High School. I was then sixteen years old. The job was that of a counselor at Crystal Lake Day Camp, which was located just next to the smallish Crystal Lake Amusement Park on Eagle Rock Avenue in West Orange. This was just opposite the renowned Pal's Cabin, a restaurant which was a favorite hangout of certain Columbia High School types, and still exists. My salary for the eight weeks of camp was $50. I don't mean $50 a week;

I mean $50 for all eight weeks! The other counselors got $75 because they were older; I was the youngest among them by at least a year. I thought that I would receive tips from the little brats' grateful parents at the end of that summer (after all, I had looked after their five and six year olds every weekday for eight weeks) but, hard as it is to believe, I got not so much as a buck from any of them.

I did not like that job at all and wanted to quit after a couple of weeks. But of course my father quite rightly would not permit me to do that; I had made a commitment and I had to keep it. As was invariably the case my dad was correct; notwithstanding (1) that the owners/operators of the camp, one Ira Kanowith ("Uncle Ira") and one Louis Siegel ("Uncle Lou") were both Newark schoolteachers earning pitifully low salaries during the year, and so they exploited their counselors by giving them wretchedly low salaries just as the Newark School Board exploited *them* by paying *them* wretchedly low salaries; and (2) that the campers' parents were generally a bunch of crude cheapskates. It has occurred to me on further reflection, however, that Messrs. Kanowith and Siegel may have told parents in writing that tipping was neither required nor expected. I doubt that, but if so I now apologize for what I just wrote about the parents!

The Marine Grill. On the Fourth of July weekend after my junior year at Columbia High School in 1948, I went to the Jersey shore, to Asbury Park with Midge Glickfeld. As was our custom in those days, we took a furnished room in a private rooming house in Asbury. In fact there were literally hundreds of such rooms rented out to vacationers at the shore in the days before motels and similar excrescences sprung up on the outskirts of all American cities and towns. After quickly settling into our room, we headed for the Loch Arbour beach. Loch Arbour is a tiny locality located just north of Asbury, on the other side of Deal Lake. The beach there was used by all of us—Pa and Nanna, we Newmans, the Carris family and many other friends and families whom we knew back in Essex County and environs. Located at the northern extremity of Asbury, with Deal Lake across the road and the boardwalk, beach and the Atlantic Ocean behind it, was a landmark restaurant named the Marine Grill, noted for its lobster, other seafood and fish lunches and dinners. One day, short-cutting across the restaurant's front lawn and parking area to reach the boardwalk and thence the Loch Arbour bathhouses and beach, located at the very end of the Asbury boardwalk, Midge and I encountered Nick Maskaleris, a slightly older cousin of Connie Maskaleris, a classmate of mine every since Tuscan school days. Through relatives or friends in the Greek community, Nick had obtained a job as head busboy and parking lot attendant at the Marine Grill, which was owned and operated by a Greek-born man whose name I cannot recall. Nick told us that he had one busboy job available. There had been two such jobs and he had just filled one of them by hiring a boy named Sheldon Gross, from Jersey City. Did one of us want the second position, Nick asked. Midge did not, but I sure did! Especially when Nick took out his wallet and showed us two $100 bills neatly folded and tucked away. These represented his savings from his days on the job just since school had ended a couple of weeks previously.

I began work almost right away. My new colleague, "Shelley" Gross, had recently graduated from "Arts High," i.e., Newark School of Fine and Industrial Arts, the principal of which was no other than Aunt Sylvia Carris's friend, Dr. Fred Seamster, a man who was always extremely nice to Joe Carris and me. Shelley was a good guy and we became good pals for that summer, after which I don't think I ever saw him again. My work schedule was 5-1/2 days a week, with 1-1/2 weekdays off. The actual pay was very low, of course, but we three busboys were given 10 percent of their tips by all of the waitresses, of which there were perhaps a dozen. All in all, I made about $60-65 a week, in addition to which I got two meals a day, breakfast and supper, at the Grill. These of course we ate in the kitchen and the food was *not* the food that the customers got. Most of the waitresses were students at New Jersey College for Women, which later changed its name to Douglass College for some reason. The waitresses were between their freshman and sophomore years in most cases, and they were certainly a very nice bunch of girls. The owner of the restaurant was called "Papa John"—*not* to his face!—by all of us except perhaps Nick.

In the kitchen, behind a long and large metal table onto which we deposited the dirty dishes we bussed from the diners' tables, were the dishwashers, some five or six bouncy Negroes, as Americans of African origin were then known. These guys were about my age or a bit older. They were a rather rough looking and acting bunch from the South whom I was a bit wary of. The fact is that I really didn't like them much and I'm sure they reciprocated this sentiment. In fact, they used to rag me and Shelley continually.

Another good feature of the job was that we had a couple of hours off in the afternoons between the lunch and dinner hours. This enabled us to go to the Loch Arbour beach for a while even on workdays. This I of course liked a great deal because it gave me the opportunity to see guys I knew and—Jeanne Barna! The fact is that it was mainly because of Jeanne, a very cute sixteen year-old blonde girl from Jackson Heights, Queens, that I so wanted to spend that summer at the shore. Her parents were divorced (*cosa rara* in those days). I always wondered if her father was related to "Babe" Barna, a New York Giants outfielder of the time. Her mother's younger sister, a very good-looking woman who was an older version of Jeanne, had married well, had not divorced, and lived with her husband in a nice house in Livingston with another nice house (a shore type cottage) in Loch Arbour a half block from the beach. Jeanne was spending the summer with this aunt and uncle. I saw Jeanne on the beach daily and had many an evening date with her after work. I was quite sweet on her, and this sentiment of mine was reciprocated by her.

My own digs were the attic of an old three or four-story wooden hotel of the Jersey shore type, a few blocks away in Asbury Park. I don't mean I had a room in this attic; I mean I had the whole attic, with either a cot or a mattress on the floor for sleeping. It had a tendency to get a bit hot up there during the day, but the nights were okay, usually tempered by a nice, delicious-smelling cool breeze off the ocean. My rent: $10 a week. When my mother saw these accommodations, she was not thrilled. In particular she was worried about fire, a potential danger with which she one day confronted the owner of the hotel, a middle-aged woman whose name I do not recall. Not to worry, she soothed my mother; if ever there was a fire, Joe could simply jump from the roof of the hotel onto the roof of a similar wooden hotel next door (probably also ablaze!)

A few other things about my Marine Grille job are worth recounting. Papa John went to the races at Monmouth Park almost every day. When he returned for the dinner session at the restaurant, we always could tell straightaway whether he had won or lost. He had a table near the doors leading from the dining area to the kitchen. This was in effect his "office." We called this Papa's Place and the waitresses even made up and sang a song called "Vive le Papa's Place", which was quite clever and humorous. The table always had at least a dozen bottles of various kinds of pills which Papa was continually popping.

One morning Papa said to me in his quite thick Greek accent: "Joey, go and pick up all ze peppers." I found this rather odd but orders were orders so I took up a tray and proceeded to make the rounds of all the tables, picking up the pepper shakers therefrom. After a time Papa noticed what I was doing and demanded: "What are you doing?" "Picking up the peppers," I replied weakly, realizing that I had got it wrong somehow. "Go outside and pick up all ze papers (which of course he pronounced "peppers") from the grass!" Ah, ho capito—or however they say that in Greek!

A final incident was the Shelley Gross affair. One busy evening at the Grille we heard a huge crash in the kitchen. Unfortunately the noise that we and every other diner in the restaurant heard was a huge tray of dirty dishes which poor Shelley had dropped. Papa had had a bad day at the track. He ran into the kitchen, screamed, "You're fired!" at the top of his lungs at the helpless Shelley and literally chased him out the rear kitchen door of the restaurant with an icepick! Nor would he take him back the next day. Shelley was well and truly fired. As for me, I stayed on until the end of the shore season, Labor Day, working with another busboy who replaced Shelley and whom I can't remember at all.

P.S. At the end of the summer, Jeanne presented me with a gift she had been working on the better part of the summer—a pair of red, blue and yellow Argyle socks!

Burry Biscuit. After my freshman year at Penn I obtained through my dad a job at the Burry Biscuit Co., located in a section of a huge former automobile factory (a company that went bust in the Depression) on Frelinghuysen Avenue in Elizabeth. The president and I believe the principal shareholder of the company was Mr. George Burry, a dynamic man whom my father had come to know through business. Mr. Burry's wife owned and operated a small chain of candy shops of the Fanny Farmer variety in and around northern New Jersey. My father in his capacity as a commercial real estate broker specializing in commercial (retail) leasing had found some good downtown locations for Mrs. Burry's Helen Elliott shops; in the course of doing so he got to know the Burrys.

Thus it was that, in June 1950, just a few days after my June final exams at Penn, I commenced work at Burry Biscuit at a wage of ninety cents an hour. I started out on the Hopalong Cassidy cookie packaging machine (eating no small number of these cookies daily), where the work was quite boring. The problem was that I had no one to talk to. I was therefore happy when I was transferred to a packing line for various other kinds of cookies, such as sandwich crèmes. I was quite happy working on this line. I was able to talk to all the girls and young women who worked there (I was nineteen years old at the time). Moreover, the line supervisor, a fellow named Ray, and another summer job guy like myself, a lad named Ernie, who lived in Hillside and was attending Drew University in Madison, New Jersey, also worked on the line. Both were very nice fellows to know and talk with. I stayed on at Burry's for a full eleven weeks, getting a wage increase to one dollar an hour during the course of the summer.

Often Mr. Burry would walk through the factory, a very "hands-on" guy (it was said that he personally knew how to make cookie dough by hand), seeing whether all the work was proceeding to his satisfaction. The factory was very busy; he had told my father that he was "fighting for production." On these occasions he would not so much as glance at me, so I am sure that none of my fellow workers knew that I had obtained my job directly through the boss. Then, during my last week on the job, the floor supervisor of the factory, a most competent woman whose name I do not recall, stopped by our line and outside of the hearing of my co-workers told me to proceed forthwith to Mr. Burry's office, which I immediately did. When I entered his big office he asked me to be seated, and then told me that I had been a good and loyal worker during my time there. He then asked me what I had learned during my weeks there. I made some answer, what it was I can't recall, but I think it wasn't a particularly intelligent one. Then he said something to me that I have never forgotten and never will. "I hope you learned what the people who work here are up against in their lives," he told me. Until that moment, of course, I had learned no such thing. But his putting it to me in the way he did brought the point home to me with great clarity. I was going to finish college and then enter the adult world with countless advantages, whereas the people who worked at Burry's were going to continue working there or in like kinds of jobs all their working lives. I've always been grateful to Mr.

Burry, a very fine man indeed, for helping me to understand what these kinds of working people were "up against" and how very, very fortunate in life I myself was. Lesson well learned!

The Jiffy Manufacturing Company. After my sophomore year at Penn, Herb Roemmele, Joe Carris and I obtained summer jobs at Jiffy, in Elizabeth. It was Herbie who found the jobs for us through some family connection. It was a well paid job with long hours. As I recall, our working hours were 7:00 am-5:30 pm with only a half-hour for lunch. However, including the ten hours a week overtime, we cleared about $85 a week, a very good summer pay in 1951.

Jiffy still exists, I believe, at the same location. At least it did the last time I passed by on Route 22 (you could see the plant from the highway, near Edgecomb Steel). The principal product was and is the "Jiffy bag," a manila-type envelope insulated with finely ground up newspaper called "batting" or "bat," used for mailing books and other fragile kinds of things.

What I can remember most about this job is how endlessly long the working day seemed to us and how precious was our all too brief lunch break from noon until twelve-thirty. At the end of the week when we got paid, however, it was all worthwhile!

Harry Kalb & Co., C.P.A. After my junior year at Penn, my summer job was at the Newark office of Harry Kalb, a country club golfing friend of my father's. Mr. Kalb was the father of a classmate, Barry Kalb. There is not much to say about this job, which was quite uninteresting, but one good thing did come out of it. It convinced me totally that one thing I surely did *not* want to be when I entered the adult working world was an accountant!

The Pabst Brewing Company. At one time in America's history there were some four thousand different beer brewing companies, a number which has of course been vastly reduced over the years. One of these, a company of considerable size and market scope, was the Pabst Brewing Company, brewers of Pabst "Blue Ribbon" beer. Pabst had a good-size brewery in Newark, just off South Orange Avenue and not very far from the South Orange line. It was there that, after graduating from Penn and before starting at Harvard Law School, I worked for about eight weeks in the summer of 1953.

This was a time when I was courting Greta Funk, whom I had met in college and whom, I was beginning to realize, I was going to marry. Fortunately the Pabst job gave me ample scope for seeing Greta in New York, where she was then working and living, quite often on those summer evenings. I worked what was and probably still is known as the "graveyard shift" and so was able to go into New York after sleeping until mid-afternoon following my midnight to eight a.m. shift at the brewery. Sometimes Greta and I would have dinner together, although I couldn't afford this often. Invariably, though, we would hit a few of our favorite New York watering holes such as Nick's, Julius's bar, and the Whaler Bar at the Midston House residential hotel, where Greta lived, located at the southeast corner of Madison Avenue and 38th Street. Shortly after 11:00 p.m., I would drop Greta off at the hotel, enjoy a few good-night kisses (of course no men were allowed on the women's floors of the hotel; I never saw Greta's room in the two years she lived there) and then drive to Newark in my 1947 yellow Chrysler Windsor convertible, punch in at Pabst, change into work clothes and begin work at midnight.

Also working at Pabst that summer was pal and cousin Joe Carris. Naturally it was great to have him around. The job would certainly have been much less enjoyable without him. Our pay was very good, $2.27 an hour, which worked out at $91 a week gross. By way of comparison, I earned $40 a week at Burry Biscuit and only $30 a week working for Mr. Kalb.

We worked on a packing line and each man on the line had three tasks which he performed in consecutive thirty minute periods. First was the pasteurizing machine. Before working at this job, I had not known that bottled beer was pasteurized, but I so learned in June 1953. My job was to stand at the "out" end of the machine where the bottles came out after the pasteurizing process; this was to assure that there were no "traffic jams" in the machine as a result of falling bottles and when there were some, to fix them. When bottles did fall over and cause a jam-up, I had to reach inside with a kind of long wooden rake and rake the bottles toward me, being sure not to knock over any other bottles while doing so. This was a not unpleasant task; in the wee hours of the night the spray of cold water inside the machine was quite refreshing. After the bottles came out of the pasteurizing machine, they moved onto a conveyor belt which carried them in a wide arc to the packing machine. At a certain point on the conveyor there was what was called an "inspection light." I had to stare at each and every bottle as they passed in front of the light and make sure that they were properly filled to a certain level and that there was no foreign matter, such as, say, Band-Aids, in them. Imagine staring at an endless stream of bottles for thirty minutes at four o'clock in the morning, especially after an evening in New York with Greta during which I invariably enjoyed a couple of drinks, often a couple of the giant whiskey sours served at Julius's, which was sort of "our" bar that summer, most cozy with its sawdust on the floor and cobwebs on the walls and ceilings.

When after what seemed an interminable thirty minutes at the inspection light, forcing myself to stay awake, I moved onto the packing machine. Well, *that* woke me up! Joe Carris or some other worker would be on the floor above (there was an opening in the ceiling above) putting cardboard cartons together, or rather into shape, slapping a paper tape across their bottoms and putting them on a chute which led down to the packing machine. At the machine I would pick up a light cardboard divider, which also came flat, put it into the square shape which just fit into the carton making twelve spaces for bottles, and then slam the container into position on the machine. I would then push a pedal with my foot and twelve bottles of Blue Ribbon would come slamming down into the carton. If the divider was not perfectly positioned in the container, then one or more bottles would break and beer would go spraying about, soaking everything nearby including me. It goes without saying that such mishaps never escaped the attention of our supervisor, who would then bawl out the "stupid kid" (me), or sometimes the "stupid college kid" (again me) for being so stupid. Absolutely mortifying it was!

How we looked forward to our three breaks during our eight-hour shift. There were thirty minutes for lunch (at 4:00 a.m.!) and two fifteen-minute slots called "relief" and "beer break." For these short breaks we went to a room referred to as the rathskeller, where free beer and Hoffman fruit-flavored carbonated beverages were available in endless supply (Pabst had bought Newark's Hoffman Beverage Company not long before my summer job at Pabst; the Hoffman bottle, a giant thing on top of the building and visible for a long way around the area, was a well-known Newark landmark).

How wonderful it was to walk out of the brewery at 0800 h. and drive to Colgate Road, where Mom had a large, delicious breakfast ready for me as soon as I arrived. Then came beautiful sleep until mid-afternoon, followed by eight or nine full hours of freedom before reporting back to work at midnight.

The Pabst job had one more great feature. When I finished work at 8:00 a.m., on Friday mornings, I would on a number of weekends drive directly to the shore, where I would enjoy a three-day weekend, not having to go back to work until midnight on Sunday. A Friday morning snooze on a beach blanket was enough for me; I had the ocean to wake me up. Also, missing a night's sleep was something I could easily do at age twenty-two. On weekends that I didn't head for the shore I would collect Greta at 5:00 p.m. in New York and we would drive to her house in Connecticut for the weekend.

That was one great summer!

So ends the recounting of the halcyon days of my Maplewood boyhood.

The schools and the kids and the mores of the times were important influences in my life.

My boyhood home, 21 Colgate Road, Maplewood, New Jersey

Tuscan School

Maplewood Junior High School

Columbia High School

Fourth Grade (Miss Cox) play, 1948

Front Row: (left to right): Patty Meeker, Pete Rommel, Norman Thomas, Joan Willits, Nancy Seitel, Walter Beaney, Anne Slater, Emily Grady, Helen Leister, Claire Hummel, _____, Sol ("Joe") Carris (in "civvies" with spotlight).

Second Row: (seated left to right): Dick Martin, Barbara Evans, Jean Szeremany, Joan Litzbauer, Mary Lou Wester, Barbara Alpaugh, Barbara Hendricks, Joanne Volz.

Back Row (left to right): Walter Rauscher, _____, Joe Newman, Herb Roemmele, Bill Clingan, Bob Moore, Ray Mutter (Behind Bob Moore), _____, Quane Risinger, Ilene Abramson, Jean Russell, Carole Taylor, Jack Bain, Dan Mishell.

"Baseball Joe," age eleven.

Eighth Grade Athletic Club, Maplewood Junior High School, 1944-45 season.

Front Row (left to right): Peter Sterling, Don Campbell, Don Ronnie, John Horbelt, Griff Amerman, Dick Martin (Captain), Bob Schneider, Quane Risinger, Ed Horbelt, Phil Smith, Ken Robson.

Back row, (left to right): Murdock Merchant, Clark Benn, Doug Hall, Jim Riley, George Cain, Ed Lipfert, Bob Wigder, Jack Quirk, Sam Farinella, Steve Miller, Dennis Morris (Coach).

Seated on floor (left to right): Bob Olwine, Bill Zwigard, Joe Newman, Dick Witzig.

Ninth Grade Athletic Club, Maplewood Junior High School, 1945-46 season.

Front Row (left to right): Tom Rehfeldt, Murdock Merchant, John Horbelt, Dick Martin, Don Ronnie (Captain), Ed Horbelt, Don Campbell, Bud Guthrie, Phil Smith.

Back Row (left to right): Bob Bolster, Sandy Scheller, Griff Amerman, Bob Wigder, George Cain, Lyle Brundage, Ed Lipfert, Pete Sterling, Bill Ottey, John Tice (Coach).

Seated on floor, left to right: Clark Benn, Bill Mataka, Dan Hopkins, Ken Robson, Bill Zwigard, Joe Newman.

Joe and Josie Kussy, circa 1910

Joe, Dottie and Rhoda Newman, 1937

Joe Newman, Joe Kussy ("Pa"), and Sol ("Joe") Carris, circa 1940.

Joe and Josie Kussy—40th anniversary party, 1939

Back Row: (left to right): (the grandparents and parents): Margaret Kussy Davidson, Dorothy Kussy Newman, Sylvia Kussy Carris, Dr. Joseph Kussy, Josephine Hertz Kussy, Al Newman, Milton Carris, Max Davidson.

Front Row: (left to right): (the kids): Rhoda Newman, Judy Davidson, Doris Davidson (in front of Judy), Joe Newman, Sol ("Joe") Carris, Ada Carris.

THE FAMILY

My family. I've written this section primarily for my children, grandchildren and, I hope, my great grandchildren.

My immediate family consisted of: my father, Albert Elias Newman; my mother, Dorothy Constance Kussy Newman; and my sister, Rhoda Jane. We were an exceptionally loving and close-knit family; those three people were very dear and important to me. But in my experience the idea of family goes well beyond immediate family members, so I'll expand this by naming the names in the several branches and sub-branches of the "tree."

Two of my maternal great-grandparents were Gustav and Bella Bloch Kussy, who came to these shores about a hundred and fifty years ago from Bohemia (now part of the Czech Republic, then part of the Austro-Hungarian Empire) and Bavaria, settling in the city of Newark, New Jersey. They had six children: Meyer, Herman, Nathan, Bertha, Sarah and Joseph. The latter was my maternal grandfather, Dr. Joe Kussy. My other two maternal great-grandparents were Isaac Hertz, a native of Germany, and Emma Borne Hertz, a native of Indiana (nickname "Shirtsie"). All their offspring were daughters: Alice, Molly, Carlotta, Fanny, Helen and Josephine, my maternal grandmother. Joe and Josie in turn had three daughters: Sylvia (the mother of Joe Carris, my cousin and lifelong dear friend, mentioned often in these pages), Margaret, and Dorothy, my mother.

I hope the reader is not too exhausted by this enumeration because next I turn to my paternal grandparents. Strangely enough, I know nothing about my father's grandparents, neither their names nor whence they came. My paternal grandfather was Harold Louis Newman, born in America. He had one brother, Nathan, founder of the Virginia branch of the Newman family (more about them later). My paternal grandmother was Dora Axelroth Newman. Again, I don't know the names of her parents or whence they came. The Axelroth family at one time lived at 514 E. 12th Street, New York, a building which still stands. In their one-floor "railroad flat," they reared seven children: Jacob, Nathan (known to me as "Uncle Natie"), Sam (known to me as "Uncle Sam from Manchester" because he lived in that New Hampshire city), Hannah, Bessie, Ethel and Dora, my grandmother. Harold and Dora in turn had three children: Albert (my father), Dan and Ruth.

Sunday evening suppers with "The Bunch." This was the name given to my father's family by my mother. On many a Sunday afternoon at our house at 21 Colgate Road, I would hear Mom announce that the bunch were coming for supper. This meant that Dad, with me in tow as a rule, would go to Sweet's Delicatessen up at the corner of Springfield Avenue and Prospect Street to get "cold cuts" (roast beef, tongue, ham, rye bread, potato salad, cole slaw, pickles, "pot" cheese and "American" cheese) for our Sunday evening supper.

Who comprised the bunch? These were: my paternal grandfather, Harold Louis Newman; my grandmother, Dora Axelworth Newman; her three sisters, Aunt Ethel Ullman (widow), Aunt Bessie (never married) and Aunt Hannah, married to Louis Schreiber; the latter couple's son George (there was another son, Frank, but he rarely came) and my Dad's sister, Aunt Ruth Newman (never married). On rare occasions, my Dad's brother, Uncle Dan Newman and his wife Elayne also joined us.

After our Sunday delicatessen supper in the dining room, all would retire to the living room to listen to the radio—Walter Winchell, Jack Benny and Fred Allen. I can picture them all, dispersed around the perimeter of the living room—three on the sofa, two or even three on the "love seat," Dad in "his" chair, someone on the other upholstered chair and someone on the desk chair which was in the room. Rhoda and I would sit on the floor and get a big kick out of it all. I recall that when Jack Benny or one of his entourage—Mary Livingston, "Rochester" or Dennis Day—got off a good line, all present would laugh heartily. How much better than television! But of course the latter is one of the two or three most destructive inventions of the twentieth century.

I really liked all of these nice people very much indeed, but I must admit to having two favorites—Aunt Bessie and Aunt Ruth.

Aunt Ruth. My father had two siblings, Dan, who was a few years older, and Ruth, a few years younger. Ruth was a great favorite of both Rhoda and myself, and I believe that we were very dear to her. She never married, and we were her only niece and nephew until Dan married Elayne and they had two daughters, by which time Ruth had known Rho and me for some ten years and more. In fact, I was her only nephew.

Ruth was a very sweet and loving person, and innocent in many ways. She worked in Newark, mostly as a secretary. Her last position, which she held for a long time, was at a certain office of the U.S. Air Force. And for a while she worked as a nurse/receptionist in the exodontics and oral surgery office of my grandfather, Dr. Joe Kussy, on Clinton Avenue.

How many good Christmas and birthday presents she gave me! She loved to give; that was part of her sweet nature. And her good sense was demonstrated by the fact that she mostly gave me books, good ones, e.g., *The Complete Sherlock Holmes, Tom Sawyer, Huckleberry Finn, Ivanhoe, The Three Musketeers, Kidnapped* and *David Balfour* (the last two beautifully illustrated by N.C. Wyeth).

I fear, though, that she led a rather empty life. She lived alone in a small apartment in Irvington. Who could have visited her there? We never did. Did she have any friends? If so, she never surfaced any of them to us, nor did she ever speak of them.

My dear mother never failed to have Ruth to dinner at our house in Maplewood virtually once a week. Rhoda and I loved it when she came. After the advent of television, she usually came on Wednesdays, which was "fight night" on television. For reasons that are not clear to me, my father liked to watch the fights. So Mom, Rho and I would continue talking with Ruth after dinner, while Dad retired to the "sun room," where the television set was located, to watch the fisticuffs on the box. Then we would drive Ruthie home to her place in Irvington.

When Ruth died in the late 1970s, she left bequests of about $10,000 each to Mom, Rho, me, Dan and Elayne, and I believe to Elayne's two daughters, Judith (who early on chose the name "Candy," later "Kandi," for herself) and Toni.

Coles Point and the Virginia Newmans. As mentioned, my paternal grandfather Harold Louis Newman was one of two brothers, the other being Nathan. Harold remained in Newark, to which his father had come in the nineteenth century, and started our Newman family. Nathan moved to Richmond long before I was born, probably even before my father was born, and founded the family we called "the Virginia Newmans." Nathan and his wife Esther, who died at a relatively young age, had two children, Sidney and Hilda. Uncle Sid and my father were very close all their lives, in the way that Joe Carris and I have been, that is to say first cousins who were also very close friends as well.

The two businesses that Uncle Nathan started in Richmond had prospered and were being run by Uncle Sid when Rho and I first got to know our Virginia cousins. Sid and his wife Helen (who came not from Virginia but from the Bronx) and their two boys, George and Eugene, lived in a large, comfortable house on Wythe Avenue in Richmond, and spent their summers in a delightful country house on a good-sized piece of land on Virginia's "Northern Neck," in a little place called Coles Point. This was located on the Machodac Creek (really not a creek but a river) not far from Stratford Hall, birthplace of Robert E. Lee and also near the ancestral home of George Washington. The house was called "Hegs Haven" ("Hegs" being an acronym comprising the first letters of the first names of the family members). It was a true paradise. It stood on a rise overlooking the Machodac, with a large lawn between it and the water. There was a long wooden pier with a deck/dock at its end, where the Newmans' Chris Craft power boat was docked during the summer months. There were also servants' quarters, because the Newmans had two Negroes in service, Lulubell, the cook, and her husband (maybe!) John, the butler and handyman. These two were delightful caricatures of Negro servants in the South during that era. Lulu was short and round and looked like Aunt Jemima before "political correctness" totally changed the latter's appearance. John was quite distinguished looking. He had gray hair and always wore a white jacket when he served meals. He also milked the cow, unoriginally named Bessie, every day, so that we kids had delicious fresh milk to drink at every meal—non-homogenized and non-pasteurized!

We Maplewood Newmans went to Coles Point for visits of ten days to a fortnight for several years in the 1940s, making some five or six visits beginning in the summer of 1943 or thereabouts. Rho and I would look forward to these trips with (as the song says) wild anticipation. It was all so totally different from anything in our experience, and we regarded these Southern cousins as wonderful people. We liked them all a great deal, with Sid and Gene our favorites. Gene was more or less our age—two years younger than I and a year older than Rho. George, being some six years older than I, was a rather remote figure who of course didn't spend much time with us kids; he invariably had a pretty co-ed from William and Mary College, his school, visiting him at the Haven. Later on, as adults, we learned that he was and is a perfectly nice fellow. But Gene became our real pal, who came to spend the Christmas holidays with us in Maplewood several times.

The trip to Coles Point was made in our family car. During the war years, this was a 1941 black Pontiac four-door sedan, and from 1946 on it was a 1946 red four-door Buick Super sedan, which we loved. Of course no cars were manufactured in the United States during the war years, 1942-45, so there was great excitement when the new post-war models came out in 1946, and getting our new Buick was a thrill for the entire family.

I well recall the shock when, entering Virginia on our very first visit, we saw a sign on the door of a gas station bathroom that stated simply: "White Only." This was something Rho and I had never seen before, and we asked for and received an explanation from our parents. When we arrived at Coles Point, we also asked Gene about this. His reply was very matter-of-fact: "Oh, the Negroes are all right provided they know their place." This quite shocked Rho and me. His comment remained clearly in my mind and interestingly, when I related this recollection to Gene (then a Richmond physician) almost fifty years later, he refused to believe that he had said any such thing!

Our final lesson on our first trip south about the status of Negroes in Virginia and other states of the Old Confederacy came on a night when we went to the movies. The nearest movie theater was in the nearby town of Warsaw. On the evening in question, Lulubelle accompanied us. When we got to the movie theater,

I received another shock: Lulu had to go upstairs and sit in a balcony reserved for Negroes only; they were not permitted to sit among the white people in the orchestra section of the house.

I thought then and think to this day that Coles Point and Hegs Haven constituted a kind of earthly paradise. The white clapboard house, with knotty pine interiors, stood on a waterfront site of several acres, complete with the pier mentioned above. The dock/platform/deck at the end of the pier was our headquarters during a good part of each day. The adults used it to sit in the sun and read or chat. It was also perfect for jumping and diving off and for one of my favorite activities, crabbing. Crabs would attach themselves to the thick poles which supported the dock. I would either reach down from above and catch them with a crabbing net, or would approach them from the water and catch them that way. I would also walk around the water in which the pier stood and scoop them up off the bottom in my net.

Most days at Coles Point would begin with a short drive to one or both of the hamlet-like town's two general stores, Godman's and Beatley's. Godman's housed the U.S. Post Office, so we usually went there. Fishing and farming constituted the livelihood of most of the men of Coles Point. The fish pier was in fact more than interesting to me; it fascinated me. Indeed, the entire locale was a source of fascination to me, quite simply because it was the first truly rural place that I, a boy who lived and grew up in a middle to upper-middle class New Jersey suburb, had ever encountered and spent time in. And it was located in the capital state of the Old Confederacy to boot, not to mention the fact that the people there all spoke with a southern accent, one that contrasted so sharply with the mid-Atlantic accent I grew up speaking and speak to this day. So the "locals" were to me a very different and therefore very interesting group of people. I should add that they were all most friendly and courteous at all times.

Rho, Gene and I got to know two of the local kids, brothers who bore the impressive (to me for sure) names of Duke and Bliz. The latter was so named, or at least so called, because he was said to have been born during a blizzard. I was skeptical about this because snow was a rare occurrence in Virginia, so I believe their idea of a blizzard was a couple of inches of snow! Duke, who eventually became a Richmond policeman, was about a couple of years younger than I and was very sweet on my sister Rho, while Bliz was a year or so younger than Duke. They were very nice lads; we enjoyed their company and spent a good deal of time with them.

Uncle Sid's Chris Craft power boat was a sure sign of unimaginable wealth! We used it often for fishing trips on the Machodac, and we usually caught a lot of fish, including perch, flounder, river trout and catfish. Once my mother of all people caught an eel! On the evenings of fishing trip days we would enjoy a delicious fish fry prepared by the admirable Lulubelle. Another delicious meal came as a result of my crab-catching activities. I was fairly fast with the net and managed to catch quite a few during the course of a day. These were kept alive at the bottom of a very large Quinlan's pretzel can. Then in the evening, Uncle Sid would prepare the crab bake. A fire was made and the can set on a grate above the fire, resting on bricks. Into the can on top of the now-writhing crabs Uncle Sid would pour vegetable oil, salt, black pepper, red pepper and other seasonings. I watched the writhing of the crabs—imagine being cooked alive!—with a certain morbid curiosity. They died quickly, I told myself, but the noises of the crabs moving about after Sid put the top on the can belied this. In any event, my feeling rather sorry for the crabs went away when it came time to eat them. They were, in a word, delicious!

On those days when we were not fishing from the boat nor otherwise occupied (e.g., on day trips to Williamsburg or to the ancestral home of George Washington or Robert E. Lee), our two families would spend lovely, lazy days on the deck at the end of the pier, swimming and, we kids, jumping and diving. The days were generally beautiful (I cannot remember a day of rain on any of our trips, although the law of averages tells me there must have been at least one or two) and hugely enjoyable.

Another interesting aspect of Coles Point was that the property next door to Uncle Sid's was owned by Dave and Hilda Newman Brown (Sid's sister). There were four Brown children: Bernice, Esther Mae, Myrna and Joey. There was about a twenty-year age span among them. Their house was a log house, a beauty. It stands there to this day, but the Newmans' charming house burned to the ground after they sold it (the current owners have built a solid brick house on the foundation of the old house). Why they sold it we could never understand. If I had been fortunate enough to own such a property, I would have sold everything else I had in the world before selling that property. Which is exactly how I feel about my "family roots" house and property, Stony Hill Farm, in Burlington, Connecticut.

Visits from cousin Eugene Newman. During the early and middle 1940s, our cousin Eugene came to stay with us at Colgate Road over the Christmas holidays. His visits to us at Christmas were always looked forward to with keen anticipation and I'm certain he enjoyed them as much as we did. It was on one of his visits to us that he saw snow for the first time. He and we loved what we called "sleigh riding," which for us involved jumping on our Flexible Flyer sleds, belly-whopper style, at the top of the Colgate Road hill and riding them down to the bottom of the street, turning off onto the sidewalk near the bottom so as to avoid being run over by cars on busy Springfield Avenue.

Gene was with us at the time of our (i.e., Rho's and my) first New Year's Eve "party." The party consisted of just the three of us. My parents were of course out at a party of their own somewhere. So we three sampled the contents—straight—of several of the bottles of spirits in my father's liquor cabinet. The result of our imbibing was a state of complete drunkenness for the three of us. I'll never forget the feeling of amazement—not to mention great fun—we experienced this first time we felt the sensation of being "looped," "bombed," "in the bag," "snockered," "out of it," "oiled," "plastered," (these were just a few of the many synonyms for the inebriated state).

Paul Feig. Paul was one of my father's good friends, perhaps his best friend. A bachelor until into his forties, he used to come to our house on Colgate Road for dinner just about once a week through the late 1930s and 1940s, with the exception of the war years, when he was in the U.S. Army, serving in Europe throughout the European campaigns. Rhoda and I quite loved this dark, handsome, mellifluous-voiced, somewhat mysterious man. Where did he live? What did he do? Didn't he have any relatives (*we* had scores of them!)? Why did he not have a wife and children like almost all other men of our ken of our father's age? In any event, he was very special to us all, loved by us all as if he were a member of the family.

After dinner, Dad and Paul would play gin rummy for a couple of hours, with stakes of a tenth of a cent a point. My father was an excellent gin player, one who did not lose very often at all. Indeed, let it be recorded that he almost never lost. The reason for this was his "card sense." He remembered not only the cards that his opponent picked up from the discard stack but also the cards which he discarded. This gave my dad a good picture of his opponent's hand. So often did my father beat Paul in their weekly games that, in later years, Paul used to remark that he put me and Rhoda through college by means of their gin games, i.e., his losses to Al Newman!

When Paul was away in the Army, we sent him packages, such things as cookies and salamis, and corresponded by means of the famous V-Mail. He sent us interesting newspapers, British and French, about the war, including a British newspaper edition, perhaps the "Express," of the day after the Normandy invasion on 6 June 1944. I can remember the headline and being struck by my first experience of British calm, phlegm and understatement. The rather matter-of-fact headline read simply: "It Goes Well." Of course I should have saved that paper, but so also should I have saved a German propaganda picture glorifying their terrible defeat at Stalingrad, which he also sent us. And, for that matter, I would have been very well advised to save all my detective cards, war cards, baseball cards, early editions of Action Comics (Superman) and Detective Comics (Batman). I actually had very early Supermans—Action No. 3 and other under-No. 10 numbers—and the Detective Comics issue in which Robin first made his appearance. Unfortunately, I saved none of these. What lack of foresight!

It was in the 1950s, I think, that Paul got married to one Bess Aboulafia, an interesting woman of Turkish-Jewish background. After that, we saw less of Paul, of course. No more weekly gin games. Paul got into his own business as a wholesale distributor of cookies and biscuits, at which both he and Bess worked very hard. They bought a house in Millburn, had two sons, whom I saw but once or twice. I don't think Dad and Mom got together very frequently with the Feigs. The last time I saw Paul and Bess was at the surprise 70th birthday party for my mom given by Rho and Jack Weiss at their home on Woodruff Road, Edison, New Jersey.

When Paul died, around 1990, Bess did not bother to inform Rho and me of his death. This was not a good thing for her to do. Rho and I, who always loved Paul both in his own right and as our father's best friend, felt very sad, and still do, that we never had the opportunity to pay our last respects and to say a final farewell to him at his funeral. But never mind that; Rhoda and I still speak often of Paul, and I think of him often as well. When I do, I picture those two dark and handsome guys seated at our dining room table in Maplewood, playing gin. I have no doubt they are still playing gin together at least once a week up in heaven.

What we ate. The kinds of meals we ate at home in the 1930s and 1940s were fairly typical of those eaten by Depression and Second World War-era, suburban middle-class families. First, I should record the fact that we rarely ate out. When we did it was, with only rare exceptions, at inexpensive places such as the Maple Restaurant, on Springfield Avenue near Maplecrest Park, or the Little House, in nearby Millburn. If there was an important family event—a birthday or my parents' wedding anniversary—we would treat ourselves (or, rather Dad would treat us all) to dinner at the excellent Tavern Restaurant in Newark, or, once and once only, at the Chanticler in Millburn.

Breakfasts at home before school were the standard American breakfast: fresh orange or grapefruit juice; hot cereal (Quaker's Oatmeal, Cream of Wheat, Farina, Ralston or Wheatena); cold cereal (Wheaties, Kix, Kellogg's Corn Flakes, Rice Krispies, Puffed Rice, Shredded Wheat, and, until the mid-thirties, Force); eggs, scrambled, fried or poached; toast with butter and jam or honey; and, of course, milk. My mother, and indeed all mothers, believed in sending the kids off to school with good meals in their tummies.

Rho and I ate breakfast in the kitchen's "breakfast nook." My father ate a bit later than we did and he insisted on being served his morning repast at the table in the dining room with a tablecloth thereon. No nooks for our dad!

During my elementary school years at Tuscan School we went home for lunch every day. Joe Carris and I had lunch at my house and his house on alternate days. This arrangement freed up one of our moms at noon every other weekday, but that's not the reason we did lunch that way. The main reason was that Joe and I were inseparable; we liked to be together as much of the time as possible. Once in a while, when our mothers wanted to go out together during the day, for example to go shopping at one or more of Newark's department stores (Bamberger's, Kresge's, Ohrbach's or Hahne's), Joe and I were each given fifteen or twenty cents lunch money to go to the White Castle ("Buy 'Em by the Sack") at the corner of Springfield Avenue and Rutgers Street. I can never forget that our two dimes bought a lunch of three hamburgers and a chocolate milk or two hamburgers and two chocolate milks.

During our junior high and high school years we "brown-bagged" it, i.e., we took lunches to school and ate them at the school cafeteria, buying our cartons of milk there (on occasion we bought our entire lunch at the cafeteria). Lunch consisted of one or two sandwiches (believe it or not, some guys ate four of them!) of the following varieties: bologna; lettuce and tomato; peanut butter; peanut butter and jelly (*not* known as "pbj" in those days); cream cheese and jelly; cream cheese and sliced olives; American cheese; and (believe it or not again) peanut butter and mashed banana. Usually a piece of fruit and/or some cookies were included in the lunch bag.

Dinners at home were good, if not culinary triumphs. My mother described her cooking thusly: "I'm a plain but good cook"—an accurate description. Her plain, good dinners, all served with potatoes and a vegetable, included the following: breaded veal chops; lamb chops; roast beef or steak (only once in a while); liver (one of the two things I absolutely refused to eat, the other being onions); chicken; fish; hot dogs and baked beans casserole (with brown sugar, and delicious!); spaghetti with or without meatballs; elbow macaroni and cheese casserole (sometimes with chopped meat too); and as a real treat, potato pancakes, garnished with applesauce. My dad and I would each polish off ten or twelve of these, while Mom and Rho managed about three each. Desserts were various kinds of pies and cakes (my all-time favorites were lemon meringue pie and pineapple upside down cake), ice cream, or My-T-Fine pudding—chocolate, vanilla or butterscotch.

What about snacks, which for most of us kids were more interesting and succulent than run-of-the-mill meals? My own favorites (one or more of these may sound rather strange to you, but *chacun a son gout*, as the French would say) were: puffed rice doused with pan-melted butter; white bread toast dipped in pan-melted butter; zwieback; Holland rusk; fresh white bread slathered with mayonnaise; graham crackers; condensed milk, eaten right out of the can with a spoon and kept in the refrigerator; and two delicious concoctions of my favorite aunt, "Aunt Sylvia cake" and "Aunt Sylvia cookies."

As I read what I have just written, I realize yet again how bounteous was the fare enjoyed by most Americans even in times of depression and world war. I think that even then I realized what a blessing and great good fortune it was to be an American. I'll express the thought as follows: God Bless America; He has done just that for well more than two centuries.

Family Chores. It is a matter of record that there was never a washing machine in our Colgate Road house. Although Mom wasn't born with a sterling silver spoon in her mouth, the one she was born with was at least silver plate. In the domain of laundry, this translated into sending out the weekly wash to Mrs. Ross's Hand Laundry, depression or not, war or not. Every week Mr. Ross would appear at our house to pick up the week's dirty laundry while returning the previous week's in beautiful fresh, clean and crisp condition. I remember that winter, spring, summer or fall, Mr. Ross was invariably harassed and sweating from the hard—and I'm afraid thankless—pick-up and delivery jobs he had to perform six days a week. I do think, however, that my Dad's and my socks were washed at home by Mom!

My sister the "pepperpot." When I was a really rabid baseball fan, in the 1940s, the term "pepperpot" was applied to certain players known for their hustle and intensity. Two such were Leo Durocher and Eddy Stanky, both of them Dodgers. I was much enamored of this colorful appellation and applied it to my sister when she was perky and full of pep, which she almost always was. On the rare occasions when she was temporarily "down" (usually over some boy or something about school) I would beseech her to be "pepperpot." That usually did the trick.

Rhoda was also a nervy little thing. Not much fazed her. Therefore I often utilized her to perform tasks which I was too shy to undertake myself. I'll recount a good example of this admirable characteristic of my little sis. Whenever I had the opportunity to do so, which was often, I would listen to Brooklyn Dodgers games on the radio, enjoying the clearly Southern, dulcet and mellifluous voice of the magnificent Red Barber announcing the play-by-play of the ball game. When the game ended, Red would do a skillful wrap-up and summary of the highlights of the contest. If it was a home day game, listeners would hear in the background Miss Gladys Gooding playing a certain tune on the Ebbetts Field organ. I very much liked this particular melody—I do to this day—but I did not know its name. One day when Mom, Rho and I were on one of our much-loved vacations in Asbury Park at the Jersey shore, as we were passing in front of the old Columbia Hotel (a wonderful wooden structure of three or four stories, built in the style very typical of shore resorts in those days), I heard that very tune being played on the piano in the hotel bar. I asked Rho to go up there and ask the man the name of the song he was playing. I myself would never have had the nerve to do any such thing. But such a feat was as nothing to my sister. She dashed up the steps and into the bar (to this day I have the clearest picture in my mind of her doing this), emerging and running back down the steps just a few seconds later announcing to me, "Twilight Time."

Family summers at the New Jersey shore. Throughout my entire boyhood, the Jersey shore was a very important place in my life. Indeed it was a place of significance to me even before I was born; my mother and father were married there at my grandparents' summer house on a beautiful June day (the 22nd of that month) in 1930. After my arrival on the earthly scene on 26 March 1931, I spent all my early summers there. My grandfather, Dr. Joseph Kussy, as mentioned before, was an exodontist/oral surgeon with offices in Newark and although the Great Depression certainly reduced his income, he nonetheless had a sufficient income throughout the Depression years to rent a spacious summer house in Allenhurst, a tiny community of large summer houses just a few streets wide sandwiched in between Asbury Park and Deal. It is of course a matter of record that a few dollars went a very long way back then. I was later told by my mother that the rent for this summer house was $80 a month.

The house was spacious indeed. Every summer it was occupied not only by Joe and Josie Kussy but by three other families and two full-time servants. The families were those of the three Kussy girls, Dorothy, Sylvia and Margaret. The Newman family, of course, comprised Al and Dottie, myself and Rhoda (who had arrived on the scene on 10 April 1934). The Carris family comprised Sylvia and Milton, daughter Ada and my dearest friend and cousin, Joe. The Davidsons were Max and Margaret and daughters Judy and Doris. Doris, one of those name-modifiers, adopted the more hip version of "Dorrie" in due course. Add those people up and you will come up with sixteen people living in the house over the summer.

On weekdays, the men commuted to work—Pa, Al and Milton to Newark, Max to Perth Amboy. Every afternoon my mother and I would drive in our car (a little Model A Ford) to the nearby railroad station to meet my dad. As he got off the train, I would run to him, jump up to be caught in his arms and lifted the rest of the way up. Then I would reach behind his ear and find tucked there—my daily Tootsie Roll! Readers certainly know that delicious one-penny chocolate candy wrapped in wax paper and bearing that noble name. I can remember to this day, some seventy years later as I write, the great feeling of love and happiness that came over me upon going with Mom to meet Dad at the station on those wonderful summer afternoons in the early 1930s. I can also picture to this day the beaming smile that lit his handsome face as he picked me up and kissed me, and as I adoringly hugged and kissed him in return. What a wonderful memory!

Our house in Allenhurst, a large wooden affair (still there as I write this), had one particularly outstanding feature, a large porch in the front and on its east side. We of course were on the porch almost all the time. People fortunate enough to have porches, especially a covered one as we did, spent much time on them during summertime in those days before air conditioning.

During the daytime, we would invariably go to the beach at Loch Arbour, a community just one or two blocks wide, located at the ocean just north of Deal Lake, which was the northern boundary of Asbury Park. Perhaps Loch Arbour was administratively part of Asbury Park. I never knew, not that it matters in the least, but we always thought of it as a separate place and quite special locale. What does matter is that it had the excellent Loch Arbour beach and the fine wooden "bathhouses" (where you changed into your bathing suit and left your clothes) that went with it. It was here that I did my first "bathing" (for that's what going in the ocean was then called) in the delightful and thrilling and huge (oh, so huge to the little boy I then was) waves of the Atlantic Ocean. And the smell of the sea! How bracing, how invigorating, how wonderful it was—and is and always will be to me. Did I love it! Didn't we all!

This is a good point at which to relate an incident which I do not myself recall but which my mother told me about. Joe Carris and I were with our mothers on the boardwalk (Asbury Park was famous for its boardwalk, about which more later). I had found a prized possession, a feather, and was playing with it. I gave it to Joe for a quick look and hold and lo and behold, what did he proceed to do with it? Why, he dropped it through a crack in the boardwalk, that is the space between two boards, onto the sand below. Retrieval was if not impossible, certainly impractical, my mother not wishing to climb over the boardwalk railing nor to crawl around in the sand underneath in search of a feather. Result: a major tantrum by the writer at being deprived of his magnificent feather.

In later years, when my grandfather no longer rented this wonderful house, my mother took Rho and me to the shore at Asbury Park for two weeks every summer, up to and including the summer of 1946. We stayed at various "rooming houses" (i.e., bed and breakfasts without the breakfast), one of which was the "Ten Broeck House" (Mr. Frank Ten Broeck, proprietor), where my grandparents stayed after they ceased renting the Allenhurst house. Usually, the Carris family did the same, Aunt Sylvia coming down with cousin Joe. These vacations were really a great thrill for us; we looked forward to and enjoyed them to an extent difficult to convey now.

Our shore routine was simple enough, but we delighted in all parts of it. In the morning we would go for breakfast to a place called Lerner's, a pharmacy having a small section of tables for breakfast and sandwich lunches, located on the ground floor of a nice apartment building. We always referred to this as "breakfast at Lerner's"; it became a family tradition. One Saturday morning I witnessed something which astonished me. My dad, who would often join us at the shore on weekend days, arrived just as we had finished breakfast and settled the bill, which probably came to about a dollar for the three of us. Having just driven down from Maplewood and wanting a cup of coffee, he sat down at the table with us and asked the waitress to bring him one. After he drank the coffee he paid the ten cents that it cost and then left a quarter tip! I think my jaw dropped in amazement at my Dad's leaving such a huge tip—half my weekly "allowance"—for just a "cuppa." But of course our much-loved father was always a most generous man. That was just part of his nature. My mother on the other hand was always quite cautious in her spending.

After breakfast we would go to Loch Arbour Beach. (One summer, however, Joe Carris and I took a fancy to the new Walter Reade salt water pool in Asbury; we would go there in the mornings and to the beach in the afternoon). This was the beach that my parents had gone to since before they were married, and to which my grandparents, Pa and Nanna, had gone for who knows how many years—with the wonderful ocean, the big "breakers," the bathhouse and the snack stand where one could get good hamburgers, hot dogs, ice cream and sodas.

Dinner would be taken early at various places in Asbury. In fact we called it not dinner but supper, and we usually sat down for it as early as 5:30 p.m. The total dinner bill for Mom, Rho and me would generally be on the order of two dollars. Most of the restaurants had special meals for children, with small portions and very low prices, always under fifty cents at the places we went to.

There were several other great features of vacations at the shore in those days. First and foremost of these was the famous boardwalk, which ran along the oceanfront from Loch Arbour to Ocean Grove (known to one and all—except perhaps the residents thereof—as "Ocean Grave" and memorable for being in effect "closed" on Sunday. That's no joke; the gates to that little place were literally closed on Sunday so that no one could drive in.) All along the boardwalk there were attractions to delight visitors and vacationers. There was: another salt water swimming pool, a smaller one than Reade's; many rides of the kind found at amusement parks; the "Criterion," a shop featuring candied apples and delicious candies, salt water taffy in particular (there were several other taffy shops along the route, at which Joe Carris and I used to gaze at the taffy pulling machine in fascination); a Taylor's Pork Roll stand (delicious!); a Kohr's frozen custard stand (also delicious!); the premises of the auctioneer Richard Kadrey (of more interest to my grandparents, Pa and Nanna, my mom and Aunt Sylvia than to us kids), who auctioned various quality items such as Oriental rugs; three miniature golf courses (expensive at fifty cents for eighteen holes); and various restaurant, snack and souvenir stands.

There were two large masonry buildings on the boardwalk, both of which extended out over both the beach and the edge of the ocean. These were the Convention Hall and the Casino. These also had various amusements and snack bars. The Convention Hall also contained a first-run movie theater, at which the big bands of the era also played. The Casino had a truly magnificent carousel, which we called a "merry-go-round" in those days. This still exists and runs to this day—at Disneyland! I mustn't forget to mention an amusement house which stood at the end of the avenue opposite the Casino. It had a large Ferris wheel and a "chute the chute," which for a nickel you could slide down on a straw mat. Joe Carris and I loved this one, and slid down again and again until we ran out of nickels. There was another merry-go-round in this place, also a beauty, which we would ride just about every day. We rarely went a day without a Ferris wheel ride too. Both the merry-go-round and the Ferris wheel cost a dime.

There were two "luxury" class hotels in Asbury, the Berkeley-Carteret and the Monterey. Of course these were only for "rich people," but we enjoyed walking around in the attractive lobby areas. It quite fascinated us that there were people who actually could afford to stay in such places!

Now here's another tale of an astonishing tip put on the table by my father. There was a restaurant on the boardwalk, just a short distance south of the Casino, just about on the Asbury Park-Ocean Grove border, called the Homestead. One afternoon we went to this restaurant, we being Pa and Nanna, the Carris family and the Newman family. When we were done and my dad had paid the bill, he astounded me by putting a dollar bill on the table as a tip. This represented two weeks' allowance for me. I had never seen this done before, so I asked my dad about it and he explained to me about fifteen percent for service. The children's menu at the Homestead was priced at thirty-five cents. I always had the same dinner: slices of turkey with gravy, mashed potatoes and peas. An adult meal ran about seventy-five cents. Coffee, hot or iced tea were ten cents. So the meal for ten people (possibly there were only two Carrises present that day) came to somewhere between seven and eight dollars. Thus the one-dollar tip.

Joe Carris and I loved to play miniature golf. In fact we played it almost every evening after supper. The fifty-cent courses on the boardwalk were too expensive, so we located and played at another course just one street back from the boardwalk, fronting on Ocean Avenue. This one had thirty-six holes and cost but a quarter!

During World War II, Asbury Park became a training center for U.S. Navy recruits. The Navy took over the Berkeley-Carteret and Monterey hotels and billeted the men there. We all loved the Navy being there; it was quite thrilling to us. We would watch the boys doing daily calisthenics on the beach, hundreds of them, and marching hither and yon in company formations. How we admired those Navy lads, who after their training at Asbury went off to man the warships in the good fight against America's enemies in what was beyond any question a just war. It is difficult for those who did not experience the war years to fully understand just how united the American people were then, and the high esteem in which we held our servicemen. As I watched the Navy men then and there, little did I realize that I would one day serve a few years as a Navy officer myself.

I am very glad that I did so; serving on an aircraft carrier (the U.S.S. Lake Champlain, CVA-39) with the Sixth Fleet in the Mediterranean was one of the great experiences of my life. The presence of the Navy in Asbury only heightened our enjoyment of our wonderful vacation at the Jersey shore. How sad, then, that the resort part of Asbury Park in effect no longer exists and that the rest of the town is quite dreadful (although I hear it's making something of a comeback now).

I should not omit the following. Between the Casino and the Homestead there was a narrow beach. This, in the northern state of New Jersey, was the only beach in the area where Negroes were permitted. It will perhaps give an indication of what white attitudes towards Negroes were in those days that Joe Carris and I, although of course feeling sorry for the people confined to that narrow and quite dismal beach, nonetheless (I regret to admit) referred to it—only out of the hearing of our parents, of course—as "nig beach." And for those interested in the psychology of dreams, I record the fact that once as a boy I had a nightmare in which I was on that beach and it was struck by a gigantic, terrifying tidal wave.

Since writing the above, I have had a couple of afterthought recollections about our Jersey shore days. There was a pony ride in Asbury which Rho and I very much liked. Our favorite pony was named "Rose Bud," like the boy Citizen Kane's little sled, renowned in Orson Welles' truly great movie.

One of our favorite attractions on the boardwalk was the game of "Sensation." Joe Carris and I played this quite often; we loved it. It involved gently rolling a ball to and over an inclined barrier beyond which were a number of holes, each with a numerical value, into which the balls would drop if you rolled them properly. This game quite fascinated Joe and me, and we got to be quite good at it, not infrequently winning little prizes for our skill.

What lovely, lazy, delicious summer days those were.

My grandfather "mugged." During his active adult years my grandfather, Pa, had several Boston Bulls as pets. I knew two of them, "Buster" and "Skippy." Buster's era was during the years when Pa and Nanna lived in their four-story town house at 82 Clinton Avenue, Newark. Skippy's era was during the years when Pa and Nanna, their three daughters married and living with their own families, lived in an apartment building called "the Ambassador," on Johnson Avenue in Newark. During the latter years, Pa used to take Skippy for morning and evening walks every day, along Johnson Avenue for a few blocks to where the South Side High School was located and then back. It is a matter of historical fact that Johnson Avenue, once a lovely street of large houses and good apartment buildings, had become part of a "neighborhood in transition" during the War years. That's the background for what follows.

It happened that, one morning during the winter of 1944-45, I was sitting at my desk in my eighth grade home room, that of Miss Wheeler, but prior to the sounding of the bell which indicated the official start of the school day's first period, when Joe Carris (who was in a different home room) came in and approached my desk. I saw immediately that he was on the verge of tears. "Big Joe" (the name by which Pa, who was his grandfather as well as mine, was known to Joe and his sister, Ada) was mugged last night while walking Skippy, he told me. I believe that was the first time I had heard that ugly word, and as I recall Joe had to explain to me what it meant. What had in fact happened was that three young men had accosted him as he was walking Skippy, had hit him hard on the head, and stolen his wallet. Those rotten swine had beaten and badly hurt a man almost seventy years old, innocently walking his dog in his own neighborhood early in the evening. Those filthy scum could have simply demanded that he give them his money; I am sure he would have handed it over without resistance. But those dirtbags had to hit and hurt him, my dear, much-loved grandfather, a great guy in every way.

I have always devoutly wished and hoped that those filthy cowards were later on arrested and imprisoned for a long time for some other violent crime. Indeed, I'm reasonably certain that such a fate did befall them; they richly deserved it.

This event had a significant impact on me and on my attitude toward perpetrators of crimes of violence. I have always believed and always shall believe that violent criminals when apprehended should be given severe sentences. I have no sympathy whatsoever for them. It is the victims of crime who should have our sympathy, and never the criminals.

"Lend me fi' cents, boy." One afternoon during the War years I went to downtown Newark (yes, one actually could and did go there in those days) on some errand or other. After completing the errand I walked up Springfield Avenue to meet my father at his office at the Herman Kussy Company, a wholesale grocery company which supplied food products to "Ma and Pa" stores all around Newark and surrounding communities. A word of explanation is appropriate here concerning my father's employment at this company during the War. He was a commercial real estate broker throughout almost his entire working life, operating independently, as his own boss rather than as an employee of a real estate firm. Happily he was always (even during the Depression) able to earn a decent living and during the post-War years, quite a good living without really working all that hard, indeed often taking one or more weekly afternoons off to play golf at his club in North Caldwell. However, during the War, the commercial real estate business became very inactive, even dormant, in his area of specialization, chain store leasing. He was thus obligated to seek other employment during those years, which he found at the company of my grandfather's brother, Herman Kussy.

Back to my narrative. When my Uncle Herman Kussy founded his wholesale grocery business in the early part of the century, the lower Springfield Avenue section of Newark was quite a decent middle class neighborhood. In fact, his warehouse was located on the very site where my maternal great-grandparents, Gustav and Bella Kussy, had lived and reared their six children during the second half of the nineteenth century. But beginning in the 1920s and continuing into the 1930s the neighborhood went downhill so that by the 1940s it was no longer a good neighborhood. And so it happened that, as I was walking up Springfield Avenue to my Dad's office that day, I was accosted by a colored boy. Readers will recall that during that era people of African descent were referred to as "Negroes" or "colored people;" it would have been both insulting to a colored person and also possibly unwise to refer to such a person as "black" or as "African-American." In any event, this boy was both older and considerably bigger than I. Nudging me in the ribs with his elbows in a none-too-gentle way he said to me, "Lend me fi' cents, boy." I said nothing but kept right on walking, and he walked right along with me. My hope was that I would reach the Kussy building and dash inside to safety, thus foiling this threatening highwayman. But I had no such luck; it was too far up the avenue for me to reach in time. Here came that elbow in the ribs again and that, "Lend me fi' cents, boy." So I reached into my trousers pocket, brought forth a nickel and handed it over to my assailant.

Did he then say, "Thank you, boy" and go on his way? 'Fraid not! What he did was to again give me that nasty elbow, accompanied by the odious "Lend me fi' cents, boy." I was therefore obliged to produce another nickel from my pocket and hand it over to the beastly fellow, who then mercifully departed. When I at last reached my dad's office I recounted the entire episode to him and insisted that we get into his car and drive down Springfield Avenue to find the culprit and retrieve my ten cents. My dad actually humored me and drove us around down there for a few minutes until I realized that this search was bound to be fruitless because obviously ol' "Lemmeficents" had gone to ground and was holed up somewhere gloating over his ill-gotten gains!

SOME OTHER MEMORIES

Boyhood Heroes
Ball games with Pa
Pizza Comes to America
Comic Strips and Radio

My boyhood heroes. I am a strong believer in the importance of heroes to kids growing up, because they play an important part in the development of character, sense of humor, sense of duty and other personal qualities which they need to form. I myself had a good number of heroes when I was a boy. In fact, there were several categories of my heroes.

First came family members, above all my father, whom I loved and admired in every way and with whom I never encountered even one bad moment, only countless good ones. How I have missed him in the years since he left us at the early age of sixty-eight (I am seventy-five as I write this). Then there was my grandfather, Dr. Joe Kussy. Because my parents and I lived with my grandparents in their Clinton Avenue, Newark town house during the first four years of my life, I became very close to my Pa and Nanna. I recount elsewhere in these pages the many things we did together. There was also my cousin Ada's (Joe Carris's sister) husband, Lee Pearl. Lee was a young man from Belmar, New Jersey, whom Ada met while still a teenager (in fact, I believe that when she and Lee were married, she was only nineteen years old). He was a fine fellow and a very good athlete in many sports, particularly baseball and track. He graduated from Panzer College in East Orange, which was a college for men (and maybe women too) who wanted to become physical education teachers (I think Panzer no longer exists). Then to add icing to the Lee Pearl cake, when the U.S. entered the Second World War, he enlisted in the Marine Corps and went to Officer Candidate School at Parris Island. Unfortunately and through no lack of trying—he wanted that commission very much—he "bilged" on the rocks of map-reading. Sent to the fleet as a third or second-class petty officer, he was assigned to the Naval Training Center at Bainbridge, Maryland, where he put seaman recruits through basic training physical exercises, right in line with his future profession. After the war, Lee became a "phys ed" teacher in the Newark public schools, where he eventually became vice principal of Weequahic High School.

A second category of my heroes were college athletes, specifically Penn football players (college baseball was then as now not nearly as important as college football). I had three Penn football heroes. First came Frank Reagan (first or second team All-American in 1940). The first time I saw this wonderful player was at my very first Penn game, which I attended with Pa (University of

Pennsylvania Class of 1898) in the autumn of 1940. I believe the game was against Navy. It was a muddy field that day and at the end of the first half Pa took me down to the field, where the Penn players (Reagan, Jack Welsh, Paxon Gifford, Bernie Kuzsynski, Capt. Ray Frick, et al.) were coming off the field to go to the locker room in Weightman Hall for half-time. Pa pointed out Reagan to me. He was resplendent in his mud-splattered jersey of the gorgeous design—white jersey with red and blue horizontal stripes on the sleeves—worn by Penn teams in that era and indeed right through my college years (1949-53) and beyond. I looked up at him in awe. Pa wasn't able to introduce me to the great Francis Xavier Reagan, but I did meet Coach Munger right then and there. And Penn won the game. It was then and there that I knew I would follow in my grandfather's footsteps and attend the University of Pennsylvania. Could it have been otherwise?

Later, during the war years, Penn had a fine running back named Joe Kane, who was something of a wizard at broken-field running, which to me was the most thrilling thing to watch in football. He succeeded Reagan as my hero, because Frank graduated in 1940. I once wrote a letter to Joe Kane. To my absolute thrill and delight he answered my letter. After Joe moved on, my next Penn hero was Anthony "Skippy" Minisi (it's possible that Joe and Skip overlapped for a year), an outstanding back.

The third category of my heroes were big league and minor league (Newark Bears) baseball players. My first baseball hero, in 1940, was Newark Bears' outfielder Mike Chartak. I needed a new hero in 1941, because Mike had moved on elsewhere. I found not one but four of them. The first two were the Dodgers' great young stars Harold Reese and Harold Reiser—known to the world of course as Pee Wee and Pete (actually, one always referred to them in the opposite order—Pete and Pee Wee). Indeed they were just about everybody's heroes. How I loved and admired these two Dodger greats and the wonderful team they played for and led to a pennant in 1941. I will recount elsewhere in these pages how I once actually met and had a catch with Pete Reiser, Pistol Pete himself, during his sensational 1941 rookie year with the Brooks. In addition to Pete and Pee Wee, I had two more shortstop heroes (I myself was a shortstop, or at least tried to be), Phil "Scooter" Rizzuto of the Yankees and Bill Johnson of the Bears, who later became a very good Yankee player himself. But to me there was nobody quite like Pete and Pee Wee.

Next came the Maplewood heroes. Bob Roellke, Columbia High School's all-state pitcher, was my number one local hero (this was when I was in Tuscan School, fifth and sixth grade years). In addition to starring for Columbia in basketball as well as baseball, he used to pitch in pick-up/choose-up games with other Columbia guys down at Maplecrest Park during summer vacations. He was, of course, one of the star players in these games, one of the "big four" who played therein, the other three being Bill Scardefield, Bill Purdue and Glenn Ronnie, older brother of my junior high and high school classmate Don "Needle" Ronnie (himself a fine varsity basketball player). One day after one of the Maplecrest games, I actually somehow got to walk home with Bob Roellke, just the two of us (!), to his house in Joe Carris's neighborhood. What a thrill that was. I observed how Bob hung his glove (I can actually picture that glove, 1940 style) over his bat, which he had resting on his shoulder. From then on, of course, I carried my own bat and glove in exactly the same way. Please understand that not only did I walk him home, but he even talked to me! Perhaps he explained how he threw his wicked curve ball.

Bob Roellke was some six or seven years older than I, probably in Ada Carris's class. I had another hero in the same age group, my pal Charley Kimmel's older brother Seymour, who as previously mentioned, had the nickname "Caesar" (or was that actually his name? I've never known). The Kimmels being neighbors, I used to spend a good deal of time with Charley on the street and at his house, so I saw Caesar frequently. He was a very friendly, handsome yet rugged-looking guy, clean-cut too. His status as a hero only increased when he joined the Marines. Caesar had two close pals who, though not in my group of heroes, perhaps rate honorable mention. They were Dick Cherry (varsity football and baseball) and Kenny Winters, a couple of pretty admirable guys in their own right.

Then there were the fictional heroes—Batman, Robin and Superman. And finally, there was a hero who was not one man but many—the U.S. Marine, fighting his way across the islands of the Pacific, bravely fighting our enemies, the Japs. I simply could not comprehend how any man could be so brave as that typical leatherneck, for whom my admiration was total—and totally justified.

Emulating and modeling my boyhood self after all of these fine men and boys did a great deal for me, meant a lot to me, helped me during my years en route to manhood. I now thank them one and all.

Ball games with Pa. My grandfather, Pa, was, throughout his life a great sports fan. He was interested in all sports, but baseball was always his favorite, and it became my favorite too. In fact I have been a baseball fan since the Detroit Tigers—Cincinnati Reds World Series of 1940, won by the Reds in seven games. I was rooting for the Tigers, led by their slugging Hall of Fame first baseman/outfielder, Hank Greenberg, whose line-up also featured Rudy York, Charley Gehringer (also a Hall of Famer) and pitcher Dizzy Trout. The Reds' stars back then were first baseman Frank McCormick, catcher Ernie Lombardi, and pitchers Bucky Walters and "Duke" Derringer. These were the first games I ever listened to, and since then I've listened to/watched certainly more than a thousand ball games on radio and television, during more than sixty baseball seasons!

Since Pa and Nanna lived in an apartment building in Newark and my family in Maplewood, we were relatively close to the stadiums of New York's three teams—Yankee Stadium and the Polo Grounds in the Bronx and Ebbetts Field in Brooklyn (these last two sadly long gone), and quite near to Ruppert Stadium on Wilson Avenue in the Ironbound section of Newark, the home of the Newark Bears, the Yankees' top farm team. Pa took me to see many games at those four ball fields. We went regularly to see the Bears (I remember that general admission tickets cost 44 cents including tax) and occasionally to see the Yankees, Dodgers or Giants. These major league games were a major thrill for me, enabling me to see many of the great stars of the 1940s, including Joe DiMaggio, Lefty Gomez, Spud Chandler, Phil Rizzuto, Bill Dickey and Tommy Henrich of the Yankees; Pete Reiser, PeeWee Reese, Whitlow Wyatt, Kirby Higbe, Bill Herman, Dixie Walker, Ducky Medwick and Cookie Lavagetto of the Dodgers; and Mel Ott of the "Jints."

The Newark Bears fielded some great teams in the 1940s and many of their players graduated up to the Yankees and to other major league clubs. Some outstanding Bears players of those years were Tommy Holmes, Frank Kelleher, Hank Majeski (the "Staten Island Flash"), Bill Johnson, George "Snuffy" Stirnweiss, Johnny Lindell, Tommy Byrne and Joe Page.

The Thanksgiving Day Game. The annual Thanksgiving Day Game against Penn's traditional rival, Cornell, was an event attended every year not only by Pa and me but also by my grandmother, Nanna, and the entire Newman and Carris families. The tradition of our going to Penn-Cornell games on Thanksgiving Day had its origin in 1899 when Pa and Nanna, having eloped, went to the Quakers-Big Red game before proceeding with their honeymoon. Pa saw every Penn-Cornell game from then on for the rest of his life. In his last few years, he watched the games on television.

To round out the picture of this wonderful grandfather/grandson combination, Pa also took me to pro football games at the Polo Grounds, where the New York (football) Giants played. If memory serves, their greats were Mel Hein, Tuffy Leemans and Ward Cuff. This last name brings to mind a delightful memory. Every Sunday in its "color supplement" the New York Daily News had full page photos of leading sports figures. I recall one such double page which showed Ted Williams and Dom DiMaggio. Its title was "Red Sox Sockers." But the story I now relate concerns a double page showing a picture of Ward Cuff kicking a field goal, the ball of course being held in place by a teammate. The title was "Ward Cuff Kicking Goal." This of course went up on the wall of my bedroom in our Colgate Road house, there joining "Red Sox Sockers," many other color photos of my sports heroes, and two or three dozen college pennants (including quite implausibly, a Vassar pennant!). Rho saw this new edition to my sports pantheon and asked me, "Who do you like better, Joey, Ward Cuff or Kicking Goal?"

My first pro baseball game. During the summer of 1940, when I was nine years old, grandfather Joe Kussy took Joe Carris and me to Ruppert Stadium to see a Newark Bears baseball game. Ruppert Stadium (named after the owner of Ruppert beer and of the New York Yankees, Colonel Jacob Ruppert) was located on Wilson Avenue in the Ironbound section of Newark, also known then as "down neck."

The Bears played in the International League, Class AA, then the highest minor league classification. (There were no AAA minor leagues in those days.) They were the Yankees' principal farm team, along with the Kansas City Blues in the Class AA American Association. Among the Bears' top players that year were Mike Chartak, Bud Metheny, Alex Kampouris (36 home runs), Hank Borowy, Hank Majeski, Tommy Holmes and George Washburn. I can actually recall the names of almost every player on that team, but I won't bother to list them here! It was a fine team that finished second that year, won the playoffs and then defeated the American Association's Louisville Colonels to win the Little World Series.

The Bears' opponents in that first professional baseball game I ever saw were the Buffalo Bisons, a Detroit Tigers farm team. I recall three things about the game. First was the thrill of my first visit to a real ball park. Second, the Bears won the game. Third, the key, game winning hit was a late-inning double with the bases loaded by Mike Chartak, who immediately became my principal baseball hero for that year. I clearly recall Joe and me standing up and yelling at the top of our lungs during Chartak's at-bat, and then even turning it up a notch when he poked his hard line drive to left center field to clear the bases. That was the first of the many thrills provided me over the years by "the greatest game ever devised by man."

Meeting Pete Reiser. One fine morning in the late spring or early summer of 1941, Charley Kimmel came to my house and told me to come over to his house that afternoon because Pete Reiser of the Brooklyn Dodgers was going to be there on a visit. I was skeptical. Could this possibly be true? Would the great Harold Patrick ("Pistol Pete") Reiser, the Dodgers' incredible twenty-two year old rookie phenom actually come to my street? Was he really so great? Well, read his 1941 rookie year numbers and decide for yourself. He led the league in batting average—.343; slugging average—.558; doubles—39; triples—17; and runs batted in—117. Pete was simply my greatest baseball hero and god and, along with Pee Wee Reese, it was he who led the '41 Dodgers to the club's first pennant in twenty-two years. Naturally the "Brooks" were my favorite team and remained so until 1957 when one of the three most evil men of the twentieth century, Walter O'Malley, moved the team to Los Angeles (the other two were Hitler and Stalin).

I did indeed go over to Charley's that afternoon and there he was—Pistol Pete himself! Charley and I actually had a catch with him in the Kimmels' driveway. Would you believe that Pete wore a blue suit, white shirt and tie? Yes, he did. I shall never forget the thrill of this meeting and catch.

The very next season, Pete ruined his almost certain Hall of Fame career by running head first into a concrete outfield wall, in St. Louis, I believe, in pursuit of a fly ball (there were no padded walls nor warning tracks in those years) and sustaining grave head injuries. He was hitting .390 at the time this happened, but ended up the year at .310. He spent the next three years in the military and then came back for the 1946 season. Although he hung around the majors for a few years thereafter, with the Dodgers and other teams, he was only a mediocre player then, and his playing days ended in 1952. He died in 1981. Pete's story was a tragic one and, to this day, whenever I think of him or hear or see his name, a feeling of great sadness envelops me.

Cedar Lake Camp. When I was about seven years old, or maybe eight, I spent eight weeks of my summer vacation from school at Cedar Lake Camp, on the Delaware River in Pennsylvania, just across the river from New Jersey. I went to this camp because my cousin Frank Schreiber, who was several years older than I, had gone there for a few years, liked it and sort of talked me into going there too. This was a mistake; in fact I was really too young for overnight camp away from home for eight weeks. I was rather homesick a good part of the time even though my parents came to visit on weekends. Indeed I can remember one occasion when, my parents having just left after one visit, I felt the tears welling up in my eyes despite my efforts to suppress them. Moreover, I didn't like the camp's activities nor the other boys, nor my counselor, one "Bernie," all that much. And to cap it off, I had a case of impetigo (along with a score or more of my fellow campers) in the bargain!

I nonetheless stuck it out for the entire two months and looking back I'm glad I did. My sister Rho tried going to Camp Leni Lenape (named after an Indian tribe which once inhabited what are now the Orange Mountains) located in the South Orange Reservation a few miles from our house, but didn't last one night. So homesick was she that the camp director had to call my parents and ask them to come and collect her!

The thing that I liked best about Cedar Lake Camp was that there was a good waterfront pool down by the river (only the older campers were permitted to swim in the river). I can still picture today, more than sixty years later, this pool, the cabins in which we campers and our counselors lived, and the mess hall.

As I think back now, I recall another thing that I didn't like about the camp. We younger campers never got to play softball. I was then just beginning to discover and learning to love baseball, so I felt most deprived that we never got to play its sister game.

Death of Lou Gehrig. On June 3, 1941, at the tail end of my fourth grade school year at Tuscan school (teacher: Miss Cox, later Mrs. Randolph), the Newark Evening News and the Newark Star-Ledger (perhaps at that time it was still the Star-Eagle; I'm uncertain about this picayune detail) carried the news that Lou Gehrig, the New York Yankees' great "Iron Horse," had died of amyotrophic lateral sclerosis—"Lou Gehrig Disease." I can recall the headline on the front page to this day: "Lou Gehrig of Baseball Fame Dies." I cut out the lengthy obituary articles and with them began my first baseball scrapbook.

What became of my scrapbook? I am sad to relate that it was thrown away, along with my baseball cards, "war" cards, baseball scorebook and other such treasures when our attic at 21 Colgate Road was cleaned out as part of my parents' move from Maplewood to 954 Morris Turnpike, Short Hills, some time in the mid-1950s.

Pizza. The reader may wonder why this subject rates an entire separate section in this memoir. But just think about it a bit and you'll realize that it does! Pizza is an integral part of the diet of tens of millions of Americans and we tend to forget that, like bagels, its mass consumption is a postwar phenomenon. Until after the War (readers will understand that whenever I speak of "the War," I am, of course, referring to the big and glorious show of 1939-45, "our" War, not the nasty little affairs the U.S. has involved itself in since then) there simply wasn't any pizza to be had anywhere in America. It was reportedly (and probably factually) introduced into American life by some of those lucky Italians who had been prisoners of war in our country and who by hook or by crook had managed to stay on in the U.S.A. after the War ended. As new residents and soon-to-be Americans, they of course wanted to make some significant contribution to our civilization and so they gave us pizza.

The first time I ever tasted "tomato pie," as it was first called, was at a place located in that particularly down-market part of Maplewood known as Vauxhall, i.e., at the western (Union) border of Maplewood on Springfield Avenue. This place we named the "shack." It was indeed just that, a tiny wooden affair built around a pizza oven with room inside for just one person, the owner and proprietor, whose name was Sal, and a six-foot wide serving shelf at which the customers stood to place and receive their orders. Sal spoke almost no English but he did understand the terms of his trade, such as "one slice," "Coke," and "Pepsi." One slice of pizza (the price of which, along with the price of a New York subway ride, is as good an inflation indicator as economists like me have been able to come up with) cost a dime in those days and the sodas a nickel. Our usual order—two slices and a Coke—thus cost a quarter, which was comfortably within the budget dictated by my weekly allowance and modest school year earnings from jobs like setting pins at the bowling alley, shoveling snow or cutting grass (summers were a different story; then we were flush from our real summer jobs at which we earned real money).

Two additional thoughts come to mind here. The first is about the round roll with the hole in the middle. No, not the doughnut—the bagel! Just as the Italians' great cultural contribution to our American civilization had been pizza, that of the Jewish people has been the bagel! Can you believe that a few years ago bagel consumption in America passed doughnut consumption? Well, it's a fact. And it's also a fact that, according to certain experts on the subject whose expertise I have great confidence in, the mass consumption bagels sold in America today are not really bagels at all but merely bagel-shaped rolls.

Another thing that came to mind as I wrote this section was something that occurred on an occasion when I was back in Maplewood a few years ago. I drove to the place where Sal's shack had been. The latter had long since been replaced at the same location by a good-size pizza and hot dog establishment presided over by a young man whom I assumed to be Sal's grandson. I sat down at the counter and ordered two slices and a Coke. After I consumed them, I put a quarter on the counter. "What's this for?" inquired the young man. I replied, "Why, that's for the two slices and the Coke. That's what your grandfather charged for this order." Was the chap amused? I'm sorry to report he was not. "Gimme three seventy-five," said he.

"Cultural" Life: Comic Strips. The comic strips, or "funnies," which appeared daily and weekly in the daily and Sunday newspapers (except, of course the New York Times), were a feature of life to which I and millions of other kids, and for that matter, many adults as well, gave our attention almost every day, and without fail on Sundays. For the record, I have composed a list of the ones I can remember, set down in no particular order: Nancy and Sluggo (originally entitled Fritzie Ritz, who was Nancy's aunt); Li'l Abner; Buz Sawyer (his fiancée was named Christie); Gasoline Alley; Barney Google; The Phantom (his African sidekick was named Lothar); Blondie (also featuring Dagwood, Alexander, Daisy and Mr. Dithers); Mutt and Jeff; Dick Tracy; Smilin' Jack (his pal was "Downwind," who only appeared in profile); the Katzenjammer Kids (Hans and Fritz, also featuring the Captain, Momma and the Inspector); the Captain and the Kids (which certainly appeared to me to be a copyright infringement of the Katzenjammers); Dixie Dugan; Major Hoople (who frequently said "Harrumph"); Judge Puffle; the Nut Bros. (Ches and Wal); Little Orphan Annie (also featuring her dog Sandy and Daddy Warbucks); Mary Worth; Red Ryder; Prince Valiant; Buck Rogers (also featuring Wilma, Dr. Huer, and Killer Kane); Mandrake the Magician; Alley Oop; the Little King; and Maggie and Jiggs. Surely the reader will think of other strips, but these were the ones that came to mind for me.

"Cultural" Life: Radio. If the comics were an important part of our parents' and us kids' daily routine, radio was even more so. So now I'll hit you with another list! Here are some of the programs that came to mind when I sat down one day to do a radio recollection routine: Jack Benny (also featuring Mary Livingston, Rochester and Dennis Day); Fred Allen (the denizens of "Allen's Alley" were Mrs. Nussbaum, Senator Claghorn ("That's a joke, son") and Titus Moody ("Howdy, Bub"); Eddie Cantor (often also featuring the Mad Russian); Fibber McGee and Mollie; the 5:00-6:00 p.m. daily serials for us boys—The Sea Hound, Terry and the Pirates; Jack Armstrong (The All-American Boy), Superman; The Lone Ranger (also featuring Tonto and "the great horse Silver"), the theme music to which was the William Tell Overture and which was on the air Mondays, Wednesdays and Fridays from 7:30-8:00 p.m.; I Love a Mystery (featuring Reggie, Jack and Doc); The Lux Radio Theater; newsreaders Gabriel Heatter, Lowell Thomas and H.V. Kaltenborn; Bill Stern (sports news); Easy Aces (Goodman and Jane), one of my parents' favorites; Kate Smith; The Shadow (featuring Lamont Cranston and his friend Margo Lane ("the only person who knows to whom the mysterious voice of the Shadow belongs"); the Green Hornet; Henry Aldrich ("Coming, Mother!"); Uncle Don ("Hello, little friends, hello"); Walter Winchell; the Damrosch concerts; Edgar Bergen and Charley McCarthy (also featuring Mortimer Snerd); Dr. I.Q. ("I have a lady in the balcony, Doctor"); Queen for a Day; Truth or Consequences ("emceed by the highly durable Ralph Edwards); Rambling with Gambling; The Sixty-four Dollar Question; Make-believe Ballroom; Milkman's Matinee; Arthur Godfrey; Amos and Andy; Information, Please; The Quiz Kids (there were three of them but the only one whose name I can remember was Joel Kupperman, the youngest of the three); The Answer Man; Baby Snooks (played by Fanny Brice); The Great Gildersleeve; Duffy's Tavern ("Duffy's Tavern, where the elite meet to eat, Archie the manager speaking, Duffy ain't here."); One Man's Family; Abie's Irish Rose; Can You Top This? (Harry Hirshfield, Joe Laurie, Jr., and I can't remember the one other); The Gillette Cavalcade of Sports (boxing matches narrated by Don Dunphy, and the World Series); and most important to me of all, Dodger games (Red Barber assisted by Connie Desmond), Yankee games (Mel Allen), Giants games (Russ Hodges) and Newark Bears games (Earl Harper). And, by the way, the radio stations on which we heard all of the above were WEAF (660), WOR (710), WJZ (770), WABC (880), and WNEW.

An afterthought. I'm not going to say anything at all about television, for the simple reason that from the standpoint of civilization and culture, I think it is one of the three worst inventions of the twentieth century. I'll leave it to the reader to work out what the other two are.

RANDOM RECOLLECTIONS

For no particular reason, I shall begin with my first haircut. This I got when we were living on Johnson Avenue in Newark. The barber's name was Mr. Stitzel. I was a bit scared by the process.

During the first year we lived on Boyden Avenue in Maplewood, my father got me a present which I absolutely adored. It was a hand-made (by an older boy, probably one of high school age) wooden rifle that shot large, wide rubber bands. The fact is that, like almost all boys, I loved toy guns.

Once during my early Tuscan school years, I had a bad case of "grippe." After I got over it, my mother took me to Lakewood to recuperate in the wonderful pine-scented air there. One evening during dinner at the hotel we stayed at, I fashioned a gun from a piece of bread. When the waiter appeared, I told him, "Stick 'em up!" He was either startled or pretended to be. There was a floor show at dinner one night. The act I liked best was two Negroes in white tie, tails and top hats, who did a wonderful tap dance.

One fine day my mother was walking up Colgate Road on her way home when a mouse ran across her path on the sidewalk in front of her. It would not be an exaggeration to state that my mother had a wholly irrational yet nonetheless very real fear of those harmless creatures. On this occasion, fearing that the mouse might return, she turned right around and walked down the street to Springfield Avenue, from where three right turns brought her to the top of Colgate Road, from which point she could safely walk down to our house. All this to avoid a possible terrifying second encounter with little Mr. (or was it Mrs.?) Mouse!

When I was in the second grade, in the class of Miss O'Neill (later Mrs. Carrigan), at Tuscan School, our class was taken to the office of the school nurse to undergo eye tests involving reading the usual chart of letters with the large E on the top line. My sub-par performance led the school to contact my mother and recommend that she take me to an eye doctor for a full examination. Sure enough, Dr. Adelman decided that I would have to wear prescription eyeglasses for reading. I recall the feeling of dismay which overcame me when I first had to put them on in the classroom. Screwing up my courage, I tried to slip them on in what was supposed to be a nonchalant manner, but I had to suffer the mortification of a few of my classmates giggling and snickering at the sight. But classmate Kenny Robson (God bless him!) sternly said to them, "It's *not* funny!" whereupon they shut up. Thank you, Ken.

I hope at least some readers of these pages remember the children's game, "Red Rover." Our class was playing it one day in the Tuscan School gym, enjoying it hugely as always. At the tail end of this particular game, I somehow managed to be the sole survivor on one side of the gym, with the rest of the class arrayed against me. I actually got through against the solid phalanx opposite!

One summer day, after playing in a Maplewood Community League baseball game at Memorial Park (Note: there was no Little League ball in those days), I was taking a drink of water from the fountain located behind the home plate backstop cage. A big, heavy-set kid named Frank Rommel, who was a year ahead of me in school and whom I knew vaguely, placed his finger on the fountain in such a way as to make the water squirt up onto my face and into my nose. I finished my drink at the fountain and, as I did so, filled my mouth with water. Then, when Frank leaned over to drink at the fountain, I spit the mouthful right onto the back of his neck. I then jumped on my bike, as did Joe Carris who was with me, and took off fast. We headed up Oakview Avenue, a steep hill (we called it "big Oakview). Because in those days few bikes had gears, and ours didn't, it was impossible to pedal up a hill like Oakview, so when our momentum was gone we had to dismount and walk our bikes up the hill. Looking back, I saw to my chagrin that Frank was walking his bike up the incline and, with his considerable longer legs, gaining on me in hot pursuit. At the top, where Oakview leveled off, I remounted and took off as fast as I could, my heart beating wildly from exertion and cold, naked fear! It wasn't long before Frank caught up with me and, grabbing my handlebars, stopped me dead. "You little punk," said he, "you spit water on my neck!" "Well," I replied, with a huge lump in my throat, "you sprayed water on my face." A look of realization spread over Frank's big features. "Well, I guess we're even then, kid." And he actually extended his hand, which I shook with concealed joy.

A few years later, when I was at Columbia High, I got to know Frank fairly well. On many a day as mentioned before I would walk from my house over to "Midge" Glickfeld's house at 729 Prospect Street. Midge's father, "Doctor Bill" (a dentist) would drive me, Midge, Donny Lester and Frank Rommel to school (they lived near Midge). Frank grew up to become a United States Marine and then a Maplewood policeman.

Early in World War II my cousin George Schreiber received his draft notice and order to report for standard physical examination. Trying to console his mother, my Aunt Hannah, a neighbor said to her that perhaps George would turn out to be "4-F" and thus not be subject to military service. Hannah, a devout, practicing Christian Scientist, replied that she had not raised her son to be 4-F but to be 1-A, that he would proudly serve his country, and that God would protect him and he would come back home safe and sound when the war ended. And that was exactly the way it happened.

One day at Tuscan School, probably when I was in the fifth grade, classmate Ray Mutter displayed to us on the school playground, before school began, a cylindrical object, about a foot long and yellow in color that he had found on the way to school. "What is that?" we asked him. "A hunk of plastic," he replied. I believe that was the first time I had heard the word.

On Rutgers Street, one street over from our own lived the Litwin family. The boy of that family, Tommy, was a Tuscan School and neighborhood friend of my sister Rho. Parenthetically, in 1955, I encountered Tommy as an ensign on the battleship U.S.S. New Jersey in Athens, Greece. I myself was then a lieutenant (j.g.) aboard the aircraft carrier U.S.S. Lake Champlain in the Sixth Fleet. Tommy's father, whose nickname was "Moe" (was his real name Moses, we wondered? No, more likely it was probably only the mundane Morris.), was something of a Lorenzo Jones (I wonder how many readers remember the 1940s radio program of that name) and as such had actually built a television set well before that invention went into commercial production. One day we were invited into Tommy's house and saw the miracle of television for the first time. It made such an impression on me that I remember exactly what we watched on Moe's incredible box—a fencing match.

Back in the 1930s and 1940s, Japanese beetles were a major problem in Maplewood and indeed all around the northeastern United States. We kids played an important role in the effort to eradicate them. All around town you could see kids with bottles or tin cans in their hands, picking beetles off leaves and flowers and dumping them into those receptacles, which were filled about half way up with various kinds of liquids which were lethal, at least to Japanese beetles. During the war years our extermination efforts reached major proportions because we regarded these beetles not only as predators to our roses and other plants but also enemies of the United States. They were Japanese! So as we dropped them to their grisly deaths in our poison-filled receptacles, we felt a high degree of satisfaction and even a certain sense of Schadenfreude, as we watched the little bugs writhing in their death throes.

In about the years 1941-44 our family had a wonderful little dog named Jiggs (after a popular Sunday comics character of the time whom I'm sure most readers of my vintage will remember). Jiggs was a mutt, with some evident strain of bull terrier, who had been given to us by my Uncle Nate, my paternal grandmother Dora Newman's younger brother. We all adored him and he in turn adored us in the way that only dogs can do. Imagine our horror and sadness then when he was poisoned and died. Who carried out the poisoning? My sister and I, and a Colgate Road neighborhood pal of Sis, one Dicky Kroner, decided to carry out an investigation. This included the interviewing of various neighbors, and a visit to Maplecrest Hardware to ascertain if anyone on our street had recently purchased any kind of poison, e.g., rat poison, in an attempt to identify the dog-hating neighbor who had done the foul deed. Our efforts were in vain, but Rho and I know in our hearts that God found a way to impose appropriate punishment on the killer.

After the death of Jiggs we acquired another dog, a black and white, tail-less mutt named Ted. Rho liked him (I didn't very much) and even composed a rather strange little ditty about him. The lyrics: "You're a good little doggie; your name is Boogie Ted (Why "Boogie?" Darned if I know, nor does Rho), and I adore my Ted." However, he was *not* a "good little doggie," but a bad one. He bit me and also one of the neighborhood kids, Judy Stahl—now Judith Viorst, the writer—and in due course ran off (no doubt fearing punishment for some other transgression) never to be seen again. Thus did he escape euthanasia at the hands of a veterinarian.

In 1943, when Mussolini and his mistress, Clara Petacci, were caught, killed and strung up by a Milan mob, there were two photographs printed side-by-side in a Newark newspaper, either the Newark Evening News or the Newark Star-Ledger. The one on the left was of Mussolini on his balcony haranguing the Roman mob at the Piazza Venezia. The photo on the right was of him and Petacci hanging upside down at a Milan gas station. The captions under the first was "Pomp," under the second, "Circumstance." I cut this out and thumb-tacked it up on my bedroom wall, thinking, "One down, and two to go."

What were the boys' and girls' rooms called at Tuscan School in the 1930s and 1940s? Would you believe "court?" Of course any reader who was there then will remember this rather hilarious euphemism. Halfway through the morning session and then again halfway through the afternoon session we had "court period," which meant marching in an orderly manner out of our classrooms and down the corridor to the boys' and girls' rooms. What did a kid do if he or she had to go outside of court period? Why, he or she was obliged to raise his or her hand and then, when recognized by the teacher, ask politely, "May I go to court, Miss _____?" (I'll fill in that blank, going from my first grade to sixth grade: Hart, O'Neill, Sinon, Cox, Hettger, Cooper.) Naturally this question was invariably greeted with muffled snickers, much to the embarrassment of the poor kid who had to ask it.

The janitress at Tuscan School was a wonderful old Irish woman named Miss McQuilken. I say "old" but to us kids that meant anything from forty to eighty years old. I'm rather sure that she was closer to the former than to the latter age. I can still picture her in her shapeless dress, bearing her mop and pail. Who she was and how she got from Ireland, where she was born, to an elementary school in suburban New Jersey we never knew or thought to inquire. But what an ever-cheerful, friendly, dear lady she was!

"Dear lady" was just about the last appellation one would apply to the Tuscan School principal, Miss Ireland. "Stern and strict" would fit much better. Boy, did she command our respect! And our good behavior; she ran a taut ship. I don't believe I ever saw her smile, although I'm sure she did so in the company of her family and friends, nor did she speak to us in a gentle, kindly manner. I'm sure she thought it was her job to assume an austere and distant attitude. She certainly did her job well during many years. I believe that she became the Tuscan principal when the school was first opened in 1925 and that she remained at her post until 1959. Our public schools of today would certainly be better and more orderly places if headed by women like Miss Ireland.

One day, I was in Matter's drug store on Springfield Avenue near Colgate Road with classmate and fellow backyard basketball player Bob Zinckgraf, whose nickname not surprisingly was "Zinky." In walked a classmate by the name of Betty, who lived in the neighborhood south of Springfield Avenue and who was reputedly a "hot number." Whether she was or not (she probably wasn't) she certainly did manage to look the part. On this particular day she was wearing dungarees (the original name of the type of trouser now known as "jeans") rolled up above her knees. Zinky's and my eyes almost popped out of their sockets, so rare and astonishing was this delectable sight. And to top if off she actually talked to us in a kidding and, it seemed to me, slightly suggestive way. Wow! I would have given just about anything to take her out on a date, but in those days I was exceedingly shy and didn't have the nerve to ask her; which is too bad, because she might well have accepted and I could have taken her to see a double feature at the Sanford Theater in Irvington, followed by ice cream sodas at Kleest's, the Maplewood ice cream and candy emporium on Springfield Avenue which we frequented.

Who was the most sensational girl in Columbia High School during the school years 1946, 1947 and 1948? Just ask any guy who was there during any of those years: Barbara Reinfelder, of course! And who was the most beautiful teacher at Maplewood Junior High during the school years 1944, 1945 and 1946? Just ask *me*: Mrs. Hellstrom, of course.

"Rhoda's dilemma." Once my sister sneaked into my room while I was out of the house somewhere, with the purpose of finding and reading my diary. I guess I didn't hide it too well because she found it. Reading through it, she came across the words "Rhoda is a problem to the entire family." Apparently she was in some kind of hot water with Mom and Dad on the day that I wrote those words and I had felt obligated to record this for posterity. Needless to say, what I had written did not please her. In fact, it no doubt made her quite angry, but she was faced with a terrible quandary. If she told our parents about the mean thing I had written about her and they remonstrated with me about it, I would of course know that she had sneaked into my room and read my private diary. Then, watch out Rho! But on the other hand how could she remain silent and not tattle to Dad and Mom so that they would "speak to me" and maybe even (she hoped) punish me? It turned out that she feared my wrath more than the pleasure of squealing on me, so she remained silent. But only for a time. In due course she found that she needed to clear her conscience and confess to me what she had done. And so she did so—in 1970!

At the very north end of the Asbury Park boardwalk, just beyond the Marine Grill restaurant and before Loch Arbour beach, there stood a three-story apartment building. There in the summers lived my great Aunt Alice Hertz Scheuer, a sister of my maternal grandmother, Nanna. (There were four other sisters—but no brothers—Helen, Fannie, Mollie and Lottie.) In this building there also lived a man whom Rho and I dubbed the "Tan Man." He sat outside on his balcony in the sun every day, reading and acquiring the deepest, darkest burnished copper color tan I have ever seen before or since.

I recall but little about my kindergarten year at Clinton School. However, there was one incident that does stand out vividly in my memory. Kindergarten was a morning-only school day; we finished school and went home at midday. One afternoon my mother wanted to see my kindergarten classroom or perhaps I told her I wanted to take her to see it. So we walked over to Clinton in the afternoon and Mom had a look at our classroom. On one of the desks, I spied a nice little model car, which I picked up and put in my pocket. Later, walking back home, I took out my newly "found" toy and began to play with it. "Where did you get that, Joey?" asked Mom. I must have replied something to the effect that I had found it on a desk in my classroom. So my mother marched me right back to the school and required me to put the car right back on the desk from which I had taken it. She of course also explained why what I had done was wrong and that I must never take anything that belonged to someone else, i.e., never steal. The lesson certainly sunk in; I remember it so very clearly as I write this.

One fine summer day Joe Carris and I were walking along the boardwalk in Asbury Park. For some reason, perhaps having to do with the fact that there were then many retired and thus older residents in or visiting that resort city, at a location on the boardwalk there was stationed a man who for a dime would take your blood pressure. Always liking and seeking a good lark (do people still use that word in this sense?) we devised a nice ploy. Out of the field of vision of this blood pressure man, we ran back and forth at speed for some five minutes, then walked slowly up to the man, handed over our dimes, and asked him to take our blood pressure. Of course after running it was very high. With a look of concern on his face, he said to us, "You're probably kind of nervous about having your blood pressure taken, right?" We assured him that on the contrary we were both totally calm and relaxed. That only increased his concern, and as we sauntered off we had a good laugh thinking about him thinking that we poor boys were definitely not going to live very long before keeling over with heart attacks or strokes!

Dr. (Ph.D. variety) Fred Seamster, the principal of Arts High School in Newark, was a good friend of the Carris family. A bachelor with no family of his own, he of course much appreciated spending occasional evenings with the Carrises. He took a great liking to Joe and by extension to me. On one occasion he took us two boys to Washington, D.C., the first time we'd ever been to our nation's capital. Another time he took us into New York—trips to the Big Town (it wasn't yet called the Big Apple) were always major events to us—to see a good movie entitled "The House on 92nd Street," about Nazi spies in the U.S., featuring Lloyd Nolan, William Eythe, and Signe Hasso. Joe and I loved that movie, and to this day I can remember the entire plot. It was of course done in black and white, not color. Why was black and white so much better than color for this movie? Darned if I know; it just was.

My grandfather, Dr. Joe Kussy, for a number of years played in a poker game with friends on Sunday afternoons. These poker sessions were held in the back of Morty Davis's restaurant on Broad Street in Newark. The game was five-card draw only, no variations permitted, and the stakes were quarter/fifty (in our games during my high school years the stakes were nickel/dime). On one occasion Pa allowed me to come along as a spectator. I watched, fascinated, for some three hours, dying to get into the game myself to test my mettle against these veterans, confident that I could hold my own. But of course there was zero chance of that.

There is an awful tendency afoot in the land today whereby children are permitted to call adults, such as their parents' friends, by their first names. The question of what my sister and I as kids were to call my parents' friends was solved very simply; we called them "Uncle" and "Aunt," e.g., Uncle Irv and Aunt Hilda, Uncle Phil and Aunt Laura, Uncle George and Aunt Lydia, to name a few. To this day I cringe when I hear a kid call an adult by his or her first name. It sounds just plain disrespectful to me and always will. Unfortunately, however, no amount of ranting and raving by myself and my contemporaries will have any more effect on this baleful tendency then our failed efforts to stop teenagers (and older!) from using the word "like" in just about every other sentence they utter!

Excerpts from my 1946, ninth-grade diary

January 1.

Sol came over and him, Gene, Rho and me had a swell time. I fell and hurt my toe and I couldn't walk. I just hopped around. It hurt like hell. I hope it isn't broken. Conny Grimm, Rho's friend, was over until 10. We told jokes, sang, ate Sloppy Joes, pretzels, candy and Pepsi Cola. To bed at 2:00. In the day . . . heard bowl games . . . at night heard NYU 66—Colorado 52 basketball game.

January 2.

Today is the last day of vacation. Too bad. My toe still hurts. I couldn't walk good. Pa took us to Moering (a doctor in Newark. Ed.) and I had my toe x-rayed. Dr. Solk said it was not broken but maybe cracked and to bathe in Epsom salts, and I should be better in a week.

January 4.

Today I went back to school. I created a sensation with my slipper (because of cracked toe. Ed.) Naturally everybody asked about my foot.

January 10.

The Athletic Club played a sophomore team. They had Szabo, Ward, MacWright, Lombardi, Koehler, Crimmins, Jones and another guy. We won.

January 11.

At night I went to the Stanley Theater with the Mishell Family. I saw "The House on 92nd Street."

January 17.

In school today in English I along with Satterfield, Dankis, Plante gave our oral discussion on *A Bell for Adano*. After school the second squad Athletic Club played a team of Schoner, Roemmele, Zinckgraf, Edwards, Sweeney, Evans, Gaukstern and Von Glahn. We just won.

January 18.

We heard the Graziano—Horne fight in which Rocky outpointed Sonny.

January 20.

In the afternoon Nanna took me to the Adams Theatre. We saw Frankie Carle and his orchestra. It was a good show.

January 23.

At night our family went to see "The Dolly Sisters" with Betty Grable, John Payne and June Haver at the Hollywood . . . P.S. While down at Matter's (a local drug store. Ed.) with Carl and Zinky I met Betty _____, a blonde. What a chunk. Her dungarees were rolled up above her knees. Then she pulled them up further. Zing!

January 24.

We went down to Matter's. Yep, she was there. We chased her around, throwing snowballs, etc. 'Twas fun indeed!

January 25.

At night Sol and I went to Lois Friedman's party up in West Orange. Barry G. and Marcella M. were there. In some weird game I had to kiss Marcella for 15 seconds. Did I do it? Silly diary. It was hot. We also danced and played the usual games, post office and spin the bottle. That was good too.

January 28.

Today I got all my mid-year test marks. In Latin 99 ½—Algebra 74 out of 76, or 97, history 94 and English 99. These were all straight A's.

January 31.

Today the second squad Athletic Club played Wallace's team. They had Wallace, Zinckgraf, Von Glahn and Lanes. We won 27-9. I made four points.

February 1.

A great tragedy occurred today. Rags, the Carris's dog, got run over and killed. Everybody felt bad. Poor Raggie, he was such a cute little mutt-irish setter (sic). At night our family went to the Hollywood where we saw "Kiss and Tell" with Shirley Temple. It was good.

February 3.

Rho bought me the new Doc Savage, "Terror and the Lonely Widow."

February 8.

After school we had a homeroom game. We played Reynolds (the name of the homeroom teacher. Ed.). (The Horbelts, Lanes, Hopkins and Huggins) and lost 40-17. I made four points. At night I went skating at Maplecrest.

February 14.

Zoe Frisch invited Sol and I (sic) to her party tomorrow night (must have been a last minute decision. Ed.). Then we have Barry's party Sunday night, and Jean's Tuesday (must be February vacation. Ed.). What a rigorous schedule!

February 24.

Last night I had bad dreams about being bombed and then trampled by elephants. Our family went to the Sanford. We saw "Weekend at the Waldorf" with Van Johnson, Lana Turner, Ging (sic) Rogers and Walt (sic) Pigeon (sic). Then we all had tea before bed.

February 27.

To Sol's for his 15th birthday supper. I gave him $1. Pa, Nanna, I, Nate Carris (Sol's uncle. Ed.) and all the Carris family ate together.

February 28.

I forgot to say all my money was stolen out of my wallet from my locker, about $1.50. Today was a gosh-darn hell of a lousy day.

March 1.

After school our homeroom played Hurley (another homeroom team. Ed.), the best team in the 9th. We only lost 43-29. I was hot! I made 16 points. How 'bout that.

March 8.

I called for Marcy at 7:30 . . . We saw "Because of Him" and "Terror by Night," the first with C. Laughton, F. Tone, and D. Durbin, and the second with B. Rathbone and N. Bruce. We held hands near the end. Then to Schraft's (sic) for sodas.

March 9.

In the afternoon Frank (Schoner. Ed.) and I went up to his girl friend's, Joan McCoy house. Barbara Kemp, her friend, was there. Then we went up to Barb's house. Her father took us and all the Kemps down to Ecker's dog and cat hospital and they got their dog, who had been given distemper shots. It was *neat* fun. I like Barbara a lot.

March 15.

We went to the Maplewood (Theater. Ed.). We saw "What Next, Corporal Hargrove" with Robert Walker, Keenan Wynn and Jean Porter. It was swell! P.S. It rained this morning.

March 17.

At night Frank Schoner and I went to the Maplewood. We saw Jack London's "Call of the Wild" with Jack Oakie, Clark Gable and Loretta Young. It was a good show.

March 19.

Gruning's (ice cream parlor. Ed.) and Mink's store (men's wear. Ed.) burned down tonight. It's completely ruined. I wonder where all the kids'll go now.

March 20.

At night was parents' night for the Athletic Clubs. Pa, Mom and Dad came and Nanna stayed with Rhoda. There were two games. Our second squad (3rd, 4th and 5th teams) played their second squad. We won something like 69-3. Playing on the 4th team I made six points, two lay-ups and a spinner. Our line-up: Hopkins and me forwards, Scheller center, and Benn and Zwigard and Lipfert (alternating) at the other guard. Then we went down to the cafeteria for ice-cream and cake. Mr. Tice gave us our letters. They're red on a black base. It was swell.

March 23.

I played softball with Mr. and Lois Stahl, Lewis, Dickey, Rhoda and Eddie. First I broke the basket on Lois Stahl's bike with a line drive, then knocked down the light dimmer from the street light, and then smacked one through McKim's storm sash.

March 26.

Guess what? Rollie Helmsley was sold by the Yanks to the Phils yesterday. Today is my dad's and my birthday. I'm 15 and he's 42. At night Grandma, Nanna and Sol came over for my birthday supper. I got 15 bucks, a wallet from Aunt Ruth, a fielder's glove and a National League ball.

March 28.

In lunch I snuck over to the village (Maplewood Center. Ed.) with Bill Clingan again. In gym we got weighed in for strength tests. I weigh 122, that's 22 pounds since last year, and I'm 5ft 4in., a 4 in. gain. Today I didn't feel so good. It all happened at lunch when we were playing leap-frog and I was down and George Cain kneed me in the head. I got a little headache.

April 2.

In gym we had strength tests. Last year my average was 154 (over-all school average for boys was 100. Ed.) and this year 151. I'm satisfied.

April 13.

Hit Parade standing: 1. "Oh What It Seemed To Be." 2. "You Won't Be Satisfied." 3. "Personality."

April 16.

Today is opening day in the major leagues. At last!

April 18.

In lunch I asked Sandy Scheller if he'd go to see the Newark-Buffalo game with me. It's opening day. He said "O.K." and we went down to the office and asked if we could call home and ask our mothers if we could go. Dr. Fisher said "definitely not." But we decided to gyp 6th period and go anyway . . . But Newark lost 8-6, damn it!

April 26.

In the morning I played a little softball with Frank, Herb, Charley, Dicky and Eddie (Schoner, Roemmele, Kimmel, Kroner and Goldberg. Ed.), but we didn't get very far. Frank lined one through McKim's attic window. So we chipped in, bought a glass, and put it in. Then Charley, Frank, Paul Marion and I ate at Ben's Diner. I had three hamburgers and a Royal Crown.

May 9.

My homeroom starting yesterday has been the office. Ma Ferguson (Miss Ferguson, math teacher and my homeroom teacher. Ed.) kicked me out of 115.

May 16.

In activities Miss Cain's 1st period class gave a play starring Jeanne Russell, Bill Ottey, Marj Mersfelder, Joan Volz, Pete Reinhard, Dick and Jeanne Szeremany, and Jane Raymond. Pretty good.

May 18.

In the afternoon I went with Sol to the Maplewood and saw "Spellbound" with Gregory Peck and Ingrid Bergmann (sic). It was swell!

May 27.

When I arrived at school today Ma Fergy greeted me with the news that I was not only getting the old heave-ho from the classroom but also from the

M.C.C. (Maplewood Corridor Committee. Ed.). So I'm through, but I can be reinstated if I improve in homeroom.

May 31.
My butch (crew-cut. Ed.), created a slight sensation in 1st period.

June 9.
I woke up this morning regretful and remorseful that I didn't kiss Carole last night, since after all I was dancing with both my arms around her and cheek-to-cheek, and she does like me.

June 13.
In gym, in our last game in Junior High, our team lost its first game of the year. But we won the 5th period championship with 7 wins, 1 loss and 2 ties. I got a hit my first time up, my 9th hit in a row, giving me 14 for 23 for .609.

June 14.
Today is the last full day for me in good ol' M.J.H. and I sure hate to leave, no kiddin'.

June 19.
At night I heard the fight of the century, Joe Louis, the Brown Bomber and heavyweight champ and the challenger, Bill Conn. What a thrilling fight. Louis K.O.'d Conn in the 8th. Swell!!!

June 21.
Today I graduated from M.J.H. and Rhoda from Tuscan. Mom, Dad, Nanna and Pa first went to Rhoda's at 8:45 and then they all—Rhoda too—came to mine. It was neat. For our graduation exercise we had a program on something about the youth of today and the future. Then we all marched on the stage and got booklets with the Declaration of Independence, the Constitution of the U.S. and the Constitution of N.J. It was thrilling and neat. I'm awfully sorry to leave the old school, good ol' M.J.H.

June 30.
At 6:00 our family heard the atomic bomb test on Bikini Atoll in the South Pacific. It was the fourth such bomb ever exploded. Was it thrilling! Its destructive powers are inconceivable. It's really rather terrifying. Thank heaven the Japs or Germans didn't get it!

July 1.

We went to the Little Theatre and saw "King Kong" and "Son of King Kong," two thrillers about gorillas.

July 4.

Mom and Dad took me and Rho to the park for fireworks. She sat with her friends and I likewise—Rehfeldt, Horbelts, Guthrie, Quirk, Douglass, and Clark Benn. It was swell.

July 9.

Today I heard the All-Star game with Dad. The American League routed the National 12-0. Keller hit a homer and Ted Williams got 4 for 4 and two homers, one off of the blooper ball of Rip Sewell, for the first homer ever hit off of his blooper pitch. Bob Feller won and Claude Passeau lost. The game was at Fenway Park.

July 10.

I read a sexy book, "Judgment Day." The hero is a character named Studs Lonigan.

July 25.

Today we went to the shore and so much happened that I have to quit you (i.e., quit keeping the diary. Ed.). Today is Thursday the 25th and I've been having one of the best, eventful times of my life. I'll be reading you in the future. So long, Joe Newman.